THE PENGUIN GUIDE TO THE
UNITED STATES CONSTITUTION

RICHARD BEEMAN, currently a professor of history at the
University of Pennsylvania, has previously served as
the chair of the Department of History, associate dean
in Penn's School of Arts and Sciences, and dean of the
College of Arts and Sciences. He serves as a trustee of
the National Constitution Center and is chair of the
Constitution Center's Committee on Programs, Exhibits,
and Education. Author of six previous books, Professor
Beeman has received numerous grants and awards, including fellowships from the National Endowment for
the Humanities, the Rockefeller Foundation, the
Institute for Advanced Study at Princeton, and the
Huntington Library. His biography of Patrick Henry
was a finalist for the National Book Award. He is, most
recently, the author of *Plain, Honest Men: The Making
of the American Constitution.*

THE PENGUIN GUIDE TO THE UNITED STATES CONSTITUTION

*A Fully Annotated
Declaration of Independence,
U.S. Constitution and Amendments,
and Selections from*
The Federalist Papers

RICHARD BEEMAN

PENGUIN BOOKS

PENGUIN BOOKS

Published by the Penguin Group

Penguin Group (USA) Inc., 375 Hudson Street, New York, New York 10014, U.S.A.

Penguin Group (Canada), 90 Eglinton Avenue East, Suite 700, Toronto, Ontario,
Canada M4P 2Y3 (a division of Pearson Penguin Canada Inc.)

Penguin Books Ltd, 80 Strand, London WC2R 0RL, England

Penguin Ireland, 25 St Stephen's Green, Dublin 2, Ireland (a division of Penguin
Books Ltd)

Penguin Group (Australia), 250 Camberwell Road, Camberwell, Victoria 3124,
Australia (a division of Pearson Australia Group Pty Ltd)

Penguin Books India Pvt Ltd, 11 Community Centre, Panchsheel Park,
New Delhi – 110 017, India

Penguin Group (NZ), 67 Apollo Drive, Rosedale, North Shore 0632, New Zealand
(a division of Pearson New Zealand Ltd)

Penguin Books (South Africa) (Pty) Ltd, 24 Sturdee Avenue, Rosebank,
Johannesburg 2196, South Africa

Penguin Books Ltd, Registered Offices:
80 Strand, London WC2R 0RL, England

First published in Penguin Books 2010

7   9   10   8

Copyright © Richard Beeman, 2010
All rights reserved

LIBRARY OF CONGRESS CATALOGING IN PUBLICATION DATA
The Penguin guide to the United States Constitution : a fully annotated
Declaration of Independence, U.S. Constitution and amendments, and selections
from The Federalist Papers / Richard Beeman.
p.   cm.
ISBN 978-0-14-311810-7
1. Constitutional history—United States.   2. Constitutional history—United
States—Sources.   I. Beeman, Richard R.   II. Penguin Books USA, Inc.
III. Title: Guide to the United States Constitution.   IV. Title: United States
Constitution.
KF4541.P46 2010
342.7302'9—dc22   2010015820

Printed in the United States of America
Set in Walbaum MT
Designed by BTDNYC

CONTENTS

Chapter One

Chapter Two

A NOTE ON THE TEXT

THE TEXTS IN THIS EDITION ARE BASED on the transcriptions of the Declaration of Independence and the U.S. Constitution in the National Archives and Records Administration and on Jacob E. Cooke's edition of *The Federalist Papers*. In some cases the punctuation in the documents reprinted in this edition has been altered for purposes of consistency and clarity; the eighteenth-century spelling in the original documents has been retained. Following the practice in Jacob E. Cooke's *The Federalist*, the Penguin edition omits the original titles in each of the three essays reproduced from *The Federalist Papers*.

THE
PENGUIN GUIDE
TO THE UNITED STATES
CONSTITUTION

THE
DECLARATION OF
INDEPENDENCE

WHEN IN THE COURSE OF HUMAN EVENTS, it becomes necessary for one people to dissolve the political bands which have connected them with another, and to assume among the powers of the earth, the separate and equal station to which the Laws of Nature and of Nature's God entitle them, a decent respect to the opinions of mankind requires that they should declare the causes which impel them to the separation.

☞ This single opening sentence of the preamble to the Declaration of Independence displays brilliantly the ability of the document's principal author, Thomas Jefferson, to convey a wealth of meaning in just a few elegant words. It announces the Americans' intention of declaring their independence, of dissolving "the political bands" that had connected them to England. The justification for this extraordinary act was to be found in "the Laws of Nature and of Nature's God." Jefferson, a deist who did not believe that God played an active hand in the affairs of mankind, nevertheless did believe that certain natural laws were God-given. This first sentence also signals Jefferson's awareness that a compelling public statement of the reasons for the decision to seek independence from England was necessary if America's political leaders were going to earn the support not only of the people of their own colonies but, equally important, of foreign nations like France, whose support for the American military effort against England was considered crucial. Before declaring those "causes which impel them to separation," however, Jefferson lays out the general philosophy on which America's quest for independence was founded.

We hold these truths to be self-evident, that all men are created equal, that they are endowed by their Creator with certain unalienable Rights, that among these are Life, Liberty and the pursuit of Happiness.—That to secure these rights Governments are instituted among Men, deriving their just powers from the consent of the governed.—That whenever any Form of Government becomes destructive of these ends, it is the Right of the People to alter or to abolish it, and to institute new Government, laying its foundation on such principles and organizing its powers in such form, as to them shall seem most likely to effect their Safety and Happiness.

☞ The ideas embodied in the powerful opening lines of the second paragraph of the Declaration were not Jefferson's alone. The late seventeenth-century English political philosopher John Locke had written in his *Second Treatise of Civil Government* that "life, liberty, and estate" were among the "natural rights" of mankind; they were rights that existed even before governments were created, at a time when mankind was living in a "state of nature." Jefferson's fellow Virginian George Mason, again following Locke, had included in the preamble of the Virginia Declaration of Rights, penned just a few weeks before Jefferson wrote the Declaration of Independence, "That all men are by nature equally free and independent and have certain inherent rights," which he described as "the enjoyment of life and liberty, with the means of acquiring and possessing property, and pursuing and obtaining happiness and safety." But Jefferson's language has more forceful simplicity. The assertion that "all men are created equal" was in 1776 more an as-yet-unfulfilled promise than a statement of political fact, but it has helped to define some of the highest aspirations of the American nation throughout its history.

The opening lines of the second paragraph were, in fact, merely a preface to the real punch line of that paragraph: the assertion of the right to rebel against the government of England. Jefferson reminds his audience that the very purpose of government is to protect the natural rights of mankind. Since governments, at the time of their creation, base their authority on the consent of the people whom they are governing, then it is also the right of the people "to alter or to abolish" that government if its actions threaten the very liberties it was created to protect. Realizing the dangers of living in a society *without government*, Jefferson was quick to add that once the people had severed their connection with their government, they must move to form new governments whose principles and powers would be supportive of the people's "Safety and Happiness."

Prudence, indeed, will dictate, that Governments long established should not be changed for light and transient causes; and accordingly all experience hath shewn, that mankind are more disposed to suffer, while evils are sufferable, than to right themselves by abolishing the forms to which they are accustomed. But when a long train of abuses and usurpations pursuing invariably the same Object evinces a design to reduce them under absolute Despotism, it is their right, it is their duty, to throw off such Government, and to provide new Guards for their future security.—Such has been the patient sufferance of these Colonies; and such is now the necessity which constrains them to alter their former Systems of Government. The history of the present King of Great Britain is a history of repeated injuries and usurpations, all having in direct object the establishment of an absolute Tyranny over these States. To prove this, let Facts be submitted to a candid world.

👉 The men representing their colonies in the Second Continental Congress had reached the decision to declare independence reluctantly, even painfully. They had a deep reverence for English common law and indeed for the body of law and custom that they called the "English constitution." And nearly up to the moment of independence, many of those leaders expressed great affection for the institution of the monarchy. For all those reasons, the men who endorsed the Declaration of Independence wished to emphasize that their decision was not one arrived at rashly—that they had done everything within their power to find some alternative to the decision to revolt against the authority of the Crown, and that only the "long train of abuses" and the "repeated injuries and usurpations" committed by King George III had driven them to this final, decisive action.

Although Jefferson and those endorsing his Declaration were no doubt sincere in their protestations that independence was only a last resort after all other peaceful means of protecting their liberties had been exhausted, the Declaration's description of the actions and motives of the English king and government is hardly an evenhanded recitation of the facts of the case. There is an element of hysteria—or perhaps of exaggeration for the purposes of propaganda—in the charge that the actions of the king and his government were deliberately designed to "reduce them [the American colonists] under absolute Despotism," or that the entire reign of King George III, an imperfect but not evil sovereign, had been aimed at establishing an "absolute Tyranny" over the Americans. But given the purposes of the Declaration—to persuade an uncertain American public that revolution was the last and best hope and to persuade foreign nations to give their aid to that revolution—evenhandedness was not Jefferson's highest priority. And so what followed was a long list—taking up more than two-thirds of the whole document—of the grievances that had impelled Americans to take such desperate measures.

[1] He has refused his Assent to Laws the most wholesome and necessary for the public good.

[2] He has forbidden his Governors to pass Laws of immediate and pressing importance, unless suspended in their operation until his Assent should be obtained; and when so suspended, he has utterly neglected to attend to them.

[3] He has refused to pass other Laws for the accommodation of large districts of people, unless those people would relinquish the right of Representation in the Legislature, a right inestimable to them and formidable to tyrants only.

[4] He has called together legislative bodies at places unusual, uncomfortable, and distant from the depository of their public Records, for the sole purpose of fatiguing them into compliance with his measures.

[5] He has dissolved Representative Houses repeatedly, for opposing with manly firmness his invasions on the rights of the people.

[6] He has refused for a long time, after such dissolutions, to cause others to be elected; whereby the Legislative powers incapable of Annihilation have returned to the People at large for their exercise; the State remaining in the meantime exposed to all the dangers of invasion from without and convulsions within.

[7] He has endeavoured to prevent the population of these States; for that purpose obstructing the Laws for Naturalization of Foreigners; refusing to pass others to encourage their migrations hither and raising the conditions of new Appropriations of Lands.

[8] He has obstructed the Administration of Justice by refusing his Assent to Laws for establishing Judiciary powers.

[9] He has made Judges dependent on his Will alone, for the tenure of their offices and the amount and payment of their salaries.

[10] He has erected a multitude of New Offices, and sent

hither swarms of Officers to harrass our people and eat out their substance.

[11] He has kept among us in times of peace Standing Armies, without the Consent of our legislatures.

[12] He has affected to render the Military independent of and superior to the Civil power.

[13] He has combined with others to subject us to a jurisdiction foreign to our constitution and unacknowledged by our laws, giving his Assent to their Acts of pretended Legislation:

[14] For quartering large bodies of troops among us;

[15] For protecting them by a mock Trial from punishment for any Murders which they should commit on the Inhabitants of these States;

[16] For cutting off our Trade with all parts of the world;

[17] For imposing Taxes on us without our Consent;

[18] For depriving us in many cases of the benefits of Trial by Jury;

[19] For transporting us beyond Seas to be tried for pretended offences;

[20] For abolishing the free System of English Laws in a neighbouring Province, establishing therein an Arbitrary government and enlarging its Boundaries, so as to render it at once an example and fit instrument for introducing the same absolute rule into these Colonies.

[21] For taking away our Charters, abolishing our most valuable Laws, and altering fundamentally the Forms of our Governments.

[22] For suspending our own Legislatures, and declaring themselves invested with power to legislate for us in all cases whatsoever.

[23] He has abdicated Government here, by declaring us out of his Protection and waging War against us.

[24] He has plundered our seas, ravaged our Coasts, burnt our towns, and destroyed the lives of our people.

[25] He is at this time transporting large Armies of foreign Mercenaries to compleat the works of death, desolation and tyranny, already begun with circumstances of Cruelty and perfidy scarcely paralleled in the most barbarous ages and totally unworthy the Head of a civilized nation.

[26] He has constrained our fellow Citizens taken Captive on the high Seas to bear Arms against their Country, to become the executioners of their friends and Brethren or to fall themselves by their Hands.

[27] He has excited domestic insurrections amongst us and has endeavoured to bring on the inhabitants of our frontiers the merciless Indian Savages, whose known rule of warfare, is an undistinguished destruction of all ages, sexes and conditions.

✎☞ The opening paragraphs of the Declaration display the talents of Thomas Jefferson as a literary stylist and a political philosopher. In the list of specific grievances, we see Jefferson the lawyer at work. It is an exhaustive—and wholly one-sided—bill of indictment of British rule in America. On the one hand, there is a monotony to the recitation of each of the twenty-seven grievances, but on the other hand, as the list of grievances accumulates, Jefferson's tone, much like that of a prosecuting attorney delivering his summation to a jury, grows steadily more belligerent, more heated in its sense of outrage at British depredations. Nor is it merely the British actions that elicit contempt; even worse is the British *intent*. The British government and the British king in particular are portrayed as guilty, not merely of bad policies, but also of proceeding with malevolent *motives*. The grievances laid out in the Declaration are not merely *constitutional;* they are also intensely *personal*.

In the years leading up to independence, the colonists directed most of their petitions and complaints at the British parliament. They often prefaced those petitions to Parliament with expressions of their pride and loyalty as British subjects and their affection, even reverence, for both the institution of the monarchy and the person of the monarch himself, King George III. But by 1776, the Americans had reached the point where they were denying that Parliament had any authority over them whatsoever. If Parliament had no authority, then why even waste time addressing that body? Consistent with its denial of parliamentary authority, the Declaration studiously avoids any mention of Americans as British subjects. It speaks of the Americans' fundamental rights as a "people," and it lays the blame for the people's travail squarely on King George III—the "He" to whom most of the grievances refer. This decision to direct their ire at the king rather than Parliament signaled the Americans' intention to affect a fundamental shift in their allegiance, to sever altogether their relationship with their mother country, as represented by the king.

Buried in the long list of grievances—seventeenth of the twenty-seven—is the complaint with which the conflict with England ultimately began, and from which nearly all the other grievances flowed: the denunciation of the king "for imposing Taxes on us without our Consent." The American insistence that the British parliament had no right to tax them without their consent provoked the first sustained colonial protests, beginning with the Sugar and Stamp Acts of 1764 and 1765, respectively, and continuing with the Townshend duties in 1768 and the Tea Act in 1773. That this particular grievance appears in the middle of the list suggests how far the Americans had come in their opposition to British control over their affairs. The British attempts to tax the colonies were an important catalyst for what would ultimately become a revolution, but they were only that; the real causes of the American Revolution went much deeper, to the very idea that only Americans themselves could be responsible for their own governance.

There were several grievances that emerged as a direct consequence of the British decision to tax the colonies. The tenth grievance accuses the king of sending "swarms of Officers to harrass our people," an accusation that no doubt refers to the British government's decision to send additional customs officers to America to attempt to collect the new taxes imposed on the Americans. The eleventh grievance condemns the king for sending "Standing Armies" to America "in times of peace." From the British point of view, the troops were sent to aid the customs officers in carrying out their duties and to keep the peace in a situation that, from Parliament's perspective, was growing increasingly disorderly. From the American point of view, however, the decision to send the troops was one of the most ominous, for it raised the specter of military despotism and made an already volatile situation even more so. Adding insult to injury, the decision to send troops to America was accompanied by another parliamentary act that ordered Americans to provide lodging for those troops—the subject of the fourteenth grievance. The thirteenth grievance, one of the most convoluted in the list, charges the king with combining "with others to subject us to a jurisdiction foreign to our constitution." Those "others" were apparently the British parliament, which in the Declaratory Act of 1766 had asserted its right to legislate for the colonies "in all cases whatsoever," and the Board of Trade, which was charged with implementing and enforcing the new taxes imposed on the Americans.

A significant number of the grievances—nine in all—deal with encroachments on the rights of the provincial legislatures of the colonies. The king is blamed for refusing to approve laws passed by those legislatures (number 1); for instructing his governors to prevent laws already passed from going into effect (number 2); for not allowing laws to go into effect unless the people give up their right to representation in the legislature (number 3); for calling the legislatures into session at times and in places that make it difficult for them to do their business (number 4); for forcing colonial legislatures to adjourn and then preventing them from doing their business, against their wishes (number 5); for refusing to call for new elections of representatives, making it impossible for new sessions of the legislatures to begin their business and leaving the colonies without functioning governments (number 6); for refusing to agree to laws establishing provincial courts, thus threatening the colonists' control over their own judicial powers (number 8); for revoking the charters of government under which the colonies operate and, in the process, abolishing their laws (number 21); and, finally, for suspending—and in effect abolishing—some of the colonies' legislatures, thereby depriving the colonies of their right to govern themselves (number 22).

It is not at all surprising that the Declaration of Independence would devote so much space in its list of specific grievances to encroachments on the provincial legislatures. Nearly all the members of the Continental Congress who signed the Declaration were members of those legislatures. They had taken pride in the independence and autonomy of their legislatures—they considered them to be American versions of the House of Commons. But as the conflict with England escalated, royal governors and other agents of the king not only threatened the independence and autonomy of the colonial legislatures but also the prestige and power of the provincial legislators themselves. The Americans viewed these encroachments on their legislatures therefore not merely as *constitutional* threats but also as intensely *personal* assaults on their prestige and dignity.

Several of the grievances deal with the imperial government's interference with American judicial processes: making colonial judges dependent on the British government for their continuation in office and for their salaries (number 9); depriving the colonists of the right of trial by jury (number 18); attempting to transport some colonists accused of crimes back to Great Britain, to be tried there, rather than in colonial courts (number 19); and protecting British troops, "by mock Trial, from punishment for any Murders which they should commit on the Inhabitants of these States" (number 15). This last grievance, which most likely refers to the trial of the British soldiers involved in the Boston Massacre in 1770, was not wholly fair. Although the British soldiers accused of killing five Bostonians in a scuffle were acquitted, they did receive a fair trial; indeed the American patriot leader John Adams stepped forward to defend them.

If the American grievances began with taxation and gradually extended to perceived threats to colonial legislative and judicial processes, still other grievances came to the fore in the years immediately preceding independence; it was these grievances that provided much of the emotional dynamic in the American opposition to British rule. When, in response to the Boston Tea Party, Parliament passed the package of acts that came to be known as the Coercive Acts, Americans faced new, and increasingly ominous, threats to their liberties. The Massachusetts Government Act had the practical effect of replacing Massachusetts's royal government and charter with a military government headed by General Thomas Gage, actions reported in the twelfth and twenty-first grievances, which accuse the king of rendering the military superior to civilian power and of "altering fundamentally the Forms of our Governments." The sixteenth grievance, which complains of British edicts that cut off American trade "with all parts of the world," was a response to the Boston Port Act, which closed Boston's port to all trade until the town's citizens paid for the tea they had thrown into the harbor. The twentieth grievance amounts to a broad-brushed, and somewhat unfair, attack on the Quebec Act. The intention of that act was to take the first steps in organizing the vast territories in Canada that England had acquired after its victory over France in the Seven Years' War. The act made no provision for representative assemblies in that territory—a step the Americans interpreted, or perhaps misrepresented, as a prelude to an attack on all representative government in the thirteen mainland English colonies.

The final five grievances on the list build to a crescendo of outrage over British actions occurring after the outbreak of actual warfare in April of 1775. The twenty-third grievance acknowledges the reality of the state of war but places blame for that state entirely on the king. The twenty-fourth grievance, with its charge that the king has "plundered our seas, ravaged our Coasts, burnt our towns, and destroyed the lives of our people," may have been technically true, for that is the nature of warfare, but it was certainly a one-sided depiction of the growing military conflict between the two sides. The twenty-fifth grievance, which condemns the king for sending foreign mercenaries—German Hessian soldiers—to help the British army fight its war to subdue the colonies, escalates the war of words still further with its charge that the whole aim of those foreign troops was to "compleat the works of death, desolation and tyranny," all carried out in a manner that was "scarcely paralleled in the most barbarous ages." In December 1775, after reading and rejecting the so-called Olive Branch Petition from the Continental Congress, King George III declared the colonies in a state of rebellion, and in support of that declaration, Parliament passed the Prohibitory Act, effectively declaring war on American commerce on the high seas and making any sailor on an American merchant ship liable to seizure and subsequent impressment into service in the British navy. The twenty-sixth grievance, with its lament that the victimized Americans were being forced to "become the executioners of their friends and Brethren, or to fall themselves by their own Hands," once again lays the blame not at the doorstep of Parliament, but at that of the king.

The final grievance in the Declaration's list, the twenty-seventh, is extraordinary in several ways. The immediate source of the grievance was the proclamation of Virginia's royal governor, Lord Dunmore, who promised freedom to any of Virginia's slaves who deserted their masters to fight on the side of the British. There is considerable irony, as well as tragedy, in the fact that it was Lord Dunmore's offer of *freedom* to slaves who joined the British cause that convinced Virginia's slave-owning class that the British were intent on robbing them of their liberties—indeed intent on enslaving *them*. Nor was it the inciting of "domestic insurrections" alone that alarmed Americans. That final grievance goes on to denounce the king for inciting the "merciless Indian Savages whose known rule of warfare, is an undistinguished destruction of all ages, sexes and conditions" to make war against white English colonists. While the king and Parliament were hardly blameless in the matter of inciting Indian violence on the American frontier, the American colonists themselves, by their relentless move westward onto Indian lands, did most of the inciting. And the description of the "known rule of warfare" of the "merciless Indian Savages" is the most shockingly ethnocentric piece of language to appear in any of America's founding documents. Thomas Jefferson, when he penned those words, may have thought that they would strengthen his fellow colonists' commitment to band together to fight the English foe, but the words would bring no credit upon the author.

In his initial draft of the Declaration, Jefferson included one other item in the bill of indictment against the king. It is extraordinary both in its length relative to the other specific grievances in the Declaration and in the passion with which it is articulated. It read:

He has waged cruel war against human nature itself, violating its most sacred rights of life & liberty, in the persons of a distant people who never offended him, captivating & carrying them into slavery in another hemisphere, or to incur miserable death in their transportation thither. This piratical warfare, the opprobrium of *infidel* powers is the warfare of the *Christian* king of Great Britain. Determined to keep open a market in which MEN should be bought & sold, he has prostituted his negative for suppressing every legislative attempt to prohibit or restrain this execrable commerce and that this assemblage of horrors might want no fact of distinguished die, he is now exciting those very people to rise in arms among us, and to purchase that liberty of which *he* has deprived them, by murdering the people among whom *he* also obtruded them; thus paying off former crimes committed against the *liberties* of one people, with crimes which he urges them to commit against the *lives* of another.

☞ Clearly, the American colonists were not innocent and unwilling victims of British attempts to impose the institution of slavery upon them. And of course Jefferson's own history as a slaveholder—he owned at least one hundred, and perhaps as many as two hundred, slaves at the time he wrote those lines—raises doubts about the consistency, if not the sincerity, of his indictment of British complicity in the slave trade. As things turned out, Jefferson's statement of principle, if that is what it was, did not survive the drafting committee's review. As Jefferson recalled, his condemnation of the slave trade "was struck out in complaisance to South Carolina and Georgia, who had never attempted to restrain the importation of slaves, and who on the contrary still wished to continue it."

In every stage of these Oppressions We have Petitioned for Redress in the most humble terms: Our repeated Petitions have been answered only by repeated injury. A Prince whose character is thus marked by every act which may define a Tyrant, is unfit to be the ruler of a free people.

Nor have We been wanting in attentions to our Brittish brethren. We have warned them from time to time of attempts by their legislature to extend an unwarrantable jurisdiction over us. We have reminded them of the circumstances of our emigration and settlement here. We have appealed to their native justice and magnanimity, and we have conjured them by the ties of our common kindred to disavow these usurpations, which would inevitably interrupt our connections and correspondence. They too have been deaf to the voice of justice and consanguinity. We must therefore acquiesce in the necessity, which denounces our Separation, and hold them, as we hold the rest of mankind, Enemies in War, in Peace Friends.

☞ Having presented its bill of indictment, the Declaration reminds its intended audience that the colonists had done everything possible to seek a peaceful resolution of their grievances, only to be rebuffed by further encroachments on their liberty. And, once again taking aim at George III, it notes that a ruler who is so deaf to the legitimate pleas of his people is nothing other than a tyrant, "unfit to be the ruler of a free people." Nor was it the king alone who had turned a deaf ear to the colonists' pleas. The Americans had warned their "British brethren" of the injustices committed upon them, but the British people as well seemed "deaf to the voice of justice and consanguinity." Reluctantly, the Americans were forced to the conclusion that "we must . . . hold them, as we hold the rest of mankind, Enemies in War, in Peace Friends." This severance of the kinship between the British subjects of the king and the people of America represented yet another step toward an irrevocable separation between mother country and colonies.

We, therefore, the Representatives of the united States of America, in General Congress, Assembled, appealing to the Supreme Judge of the world for the rectitude of our intentions, do, in the Name and by Authority of the good People of these Colonies, solemnly publish and declare, that these United Colonies are, and of Right ought to be Free and Independent States; that they are Absolved from all Allegiance to the British Crown, and that all political connection between them and the state of Great Britain is and ought to be totally dissolved; and that as Free and Independent States they have full Power to levy War, conclude Peace, contract Alliances, establish Commerce, and to do all other Acts and Things which Independent States may of right do. And for the support of this Declaration, with a firm reliance on the Protection of divine Providence, we mutually pledge to each other our Lives, our Fortunes and our sacred Honor.

GEORGIA
Button Gwinnett
Lyman Hall
George Walton

NORTH CAROLINA
William Hooper
Joseph Hewes
John Penn

SOUTH CAROLINA
Edward Rutledge
Thomas Heyward, Jr.
Thomas Lynch, Jr.
Arthur Middleton

MASSACHUSETTS
John Hancock

MARYLAND
Samuel Chase
William Paca
Thomas Stone
Charles Carroll of
  Carrollton

VIRGINIA
George Wythe
Richard Henry Lee
Thomas Jefferson
Benjamin Harrison
Thomas Nelson, Jr.
Francis Lightfoot
  Lee
Carter Braxton

PENNSYLVANIA
Robert Morris
Benjamin Rush
Benjamin Franklin
John Morton
George Clymer
James Smith
George Taylor
James Wilson
George Ross

DELAWARE
Caesar Rodney
George Read
Thomas McKean

NEW YORK
William Floyd
Philip Livingston
Francis Lewis
Lewis Morris

NEW JERSEY
Richard Stockton
John Witherspoon
Francis Hopkinson
John Hart
Abraham Clark

NEW HAMPSHIRE
Josiah Bartlett
William Whipple

MASSACHUSETTS
Samuel Adams
John Adams
Robert Treat Paine
Elbridge Gerry

RHODE ISLAND
Stephen Hopkins
William Ellery

CONNECTICUT
Roger Sherman
Samuel Huntington
William Williams
Oliver Wolcott

NEW HAMPSHIRE
Matthew Thornton

As the Declaration reaches its conclusion, it asserts for the first time that the contemplated action is one taken by the representatives of the "united States of America." And then comes the operative sentence of the Declaration of Independence: "that these United Colonies are, and of Right ought to be Free and Independent States," that they no longer have any allegiance or obligation to the British Crown or the British nation. Implicit in the final two sentences of the document is a promise whose means of fulfillment was at that moment very much unknown. The "United Colonies" were not only declaring their independence but stating their intention, as independent and *united* states, to carry out a war against one of the world's most formidable military powers, to negotiate a successful peace, to make alliances with other nations, to promote commerce, "and do all other Acts and Things which Independent States may of right do." The Americans intended not only to form independent states but also to find ways in which those independent states could unite in common cause. And to fulfill their commitment to that common cause, the Americans, in the final line of the Declaration of Independence, pledged "to each other, our Lives, our Fortunes and our sacred Honor."

THE CONSTITUTION
OF THE
UNITED STATES

WE THE PEOPLE OF THE UNITED STATES, in Order to form a more perfect Union, establish Justice, insure domestic Tranquility, provide for the common defence, promote the general Welfare, and secure the Blessings of Liberty to ourselves and our Posterity, do ordain and establish this Constitution for the United States of America.

☞ The preamble to the Constitution is a statement of aspiration—a promise to Americans about the things that the new federal government intended to achieve for "We the People of the United States." Some of the specific objects of government stated in the preamble—the establishment of justice, insuring the peaceful operation of society, and providing for the common defense—had long been understood to be the primary responsibilities of any government. The promises to promote the general welfare and to "secure the Blessings of Liberty" are more open-ended, suggesting that the government's responsibilities extend not merely to providing essential services but also to benevolent oversight of the polity. Although the words of the preamble do not carry the force of law, they have had substantial rhetorical power over the life of the Constitution.

ARTICLE I
SECTION 1

All legislative Powers herein granted shall be vested in a Congress of the United States, which shall consist of a Senate and House of Representatives.

☞ It is no accident that the first article of the Constitution deals with the structure and powers of the Congress, for virtually all of those who took part in the drafting of the Constitution considered the legislative branch to be the most important and, rightfully, the most powerful of the three branches of government.

There was broad agreement among the framers of the Constitution that the Congress should consist of a bicameral legislature. The House of Representatives, the "lower house," was conceived to be the "great repository" of the people of the nation at large, while the Senate, "the upper house," was to be composed of only the most knowledgeable, well-educated, and virtuous, who could be relied upon to act as a moderating influence on the whims of the people at large.

Section 2

The House of Representatives shall be composed of Members chosen every second Year by the People of the several States, and the Electors in each State shall have the Qualifications requisite for Electors of the most numerous Branch of the State Legislature.

No Person shall be a Representative who shall not have attained to the Age of twenty five Years, and been seven Years a Citizen of the United States, and who shall not, when elected, be an Inhabitant of that State in which he shall be chosen.

Representatives and direct Taxes shall be apportioned among the several States which may be included within this Union, according to their respective Numbers, which shall be determined by adding to the whole Number of free Persons, including those bound to Service for a Term of Years, and excluding Indians not taxed, three fifths of all other Persons. The actual Enumeration shall be made within three Years after the first Meeting of the Congress of the United

States, and within every subsequent Term of ten Years, in such Manner as they shall by Law direct. The Number of Representatives shall not exceed one for every thirty Thousand, but each State shall have at Least one Representative; and until such enumeration shall be made, the State of New Hampshire shall be entitled to chuse three, Massachusetts eight, Rhode-Island and Providence Plantations one, Connecticut five, New-York six, New Jersey four, Pennsylvania eight, Delaware one, Maryland six, Virginia ten, North Carolina five, South Carolina five, and Georgia three.

When vacancies happen in the Representation from any State, the Executive Authority thereof shall issue Writs of Election to fill such Vacancies.

The House of Representatives shall chuse their Speaker and other Officers; and shall have the sole Power of Impeachment.

🖎 The framers of the Constitution stipulated that members of the House of Representatives, the people's house, should serve relatively short terms of only two years, after which they would be required to seek reelection should they wish to continue to represent their state. The delegates could not agree on who should be allowed to vote for members of the House of Representatives, so they left the matter of voting requirements up to the state legislatures, which had up to that time set the qualifications for voters in each of the states. In 1787 all the states except New Jersey (which briefly permitted females to vote) limited the franchise to "free men" (a term usually interpreted to exclude free blacks) and most required that voters own at least some form of property. By the 1820s, most states had opened up the franchise to free white males regardless of whether they owned property. Subsequent amendments—the Fifteenth, prohibiting the denial of the franchise on account of "race, color, or previous condition of servitude"; the Nineteenth, enfranchising women; and the Twenty-sixth, establishing a uniform voting age of eighteen—served to create a common national standard for voting in federal elections.

The requirement that members of the House of Representatives reside in the state in which they were chosen reflected the belief that representatives, if they are to serve the people who elect them, must have close and meaningful ties to the communities in which those people live.

The "three fifths of all other Persons" referred to in this section is the result of the infamous "three-fifths compromise," in which slaves, though not mentioned by name, were to be counted as three-fifths of a person in the apportionment of representation in the House of Representatives as well as in the apportioning of the amount of direct taxes to be paid by each state. The three-fifths ratio was a purely arbitrary one. It was a consequence of a fundamental contradiction that the Convention delegates were unable to resolve: slaves were human beings, but by the laws of most states they were also regarded as property. The passage of the Thirteenth Amendment abolishing slavery rendered this portion of Article I, Section 2 null and void.

Although the original Constitution laid down a formula for representation based on population (and "three fifths of all other Persons"), none of the delegates to the 1787 Convention really knew what the actual population of each of the states was. The initial apportionment of representation was merely a guess, but the Constitution did provide for a census of the population to be taken every ten years, a practice that began in 1790 and has continued to the present day.

The "sole Power of Impeachment" referred only to the first step—the equivalent of an indictment or bringing to trial—in the removal of a federal official. The grounds for impeachment set down in Article II, Section 4—"Treason, Bribery, or other High Crimes and Misdemeanors"—have been subject to widely varying interpretations.

SECTION 3

The Senate of the United States shall be composed of two Senators from each State, chosen by the Legislature thereof, for six Years; and each Senator shall have one Vote.

Immediately after they shall be assembled in Consequence of the first Election, they shall be divided as equally as may be into three Classes. The Seats of the Senators of the first Class shall be vacated at the Expiration of the second Year, of the second Class at the Expiration of the fourth Year, and of the third Class at the Expiration of the sixth Year, so that one third may be chosen every second Year; and if Vacancies happen by Resignation, or otherwise, during the Recess of the Legislature of any State, the Executive thereof may make temporary Appointments until the next Meeting of the Legislature, which shall then fill such Vacancies.

No person shall be a Senator who shall not have attained to the Age of thirty Years, and been nine Years a Citizen of the United States, and who shall not, when elected, be an Inhabitant of that State for which he shall be chosen.

The Vice President of the United States shall be President of the Senate, but shall have no Vote, unless they be equally divided.

The Senate shall chuse their other Officers, and also a President pro tempore, in the Absence of the Vice President, or when he shall exercise the Office of President of the United States.

The Senate shall have the sole Power to try all Impeachments. When sitting for that Purpose, they shall be on Oath or Affirmation. When the President of the United States is tried, the Chief Justice shall preside: And no Person shall be convicted without the Concurrence of two thirds of the Members present.

Judgment in Cases of Impeachment shall not extend further than to removal from Office, and disqualification to hold and enjoy any Office of honor, Trust or Profit under the United States: but the Party convicted shall nevertheless be liable and subject to Indictment, Trial, Judgment and Punishment, according to Law.

☞ The Senate, as the "upper house," was conceived as a more deliberative body, whose members would be comprised of the most virtuous and knowledgeable citizens in the land. The framers of the Constitution believed that Senators should therefore serve longer terms in order that they might be better insulated from the immediate pressures of public opinion. One of the means by which Senators would be protected from popular whims was to provide for an indirect method for their election, with the legislatures of the individual states being given the power over such election. The provision for staggered terms of service was designed to prevent sudden, convulsive turnover in the membership of the Senate.

Consistent with the view that the members of the Senate were expected to possess superior knowledge and experience, the minimum age of Senators was set at thirty, and the length of time after becoming a citizen nine years, as opposed to twenty-five years of age and seven years of citizenship for members of the House of Representatives.

The framers of the Constitution were aware of the necessity of providing for a vice president, who would assume the president's duties in the event of his death, disability, or removal, but they had a hard time thinking of any other functions the vice president might perform. The provision of Article I, Section 2, designating the vice president as the presiding officer of the Senate, is the only item in the Constitution that speaks to the limited official duties of the vice president.

The Senate, as the more deliberative of the two legislative bodies, was given the responsibility of trying impeachment cases. Seeking to reinforce the principle of separation of powers, the

Constitution designates the chief justice of the U.S. Supreme Court as the person who would preside over an impeachment trial of the president.

Section 4

The Times, Places and Manner of holding Elections for Senators and Representatives, shall be prescribed in each State by the Legislature thereof; but the Congress may at any time by Law make or alter such Regulations, except as to the Place of chusing Senators.

The Congress shall assemble at least once in every Year, and such Meeting shall be on the first Monday in December, unless they shall by Law appoint a different Day.

☞ As was the case in the instance of voting requirements, the framers of the Constitution were content to leave the matter of when congressional elections should be held to the state governments.

The stipulation that Congress should assemble on the first Monday in December was altered by the passage of the Twentieth Amendment in 1933. The practical effect of the original terms of Article I, Section 4, was to delay the seating of new members of Congress until March, creating a period of months during which a lame-duck Congress would be in session. Improvements in transportation and communications made it possible, and desirable, to move the stipulated time of the meeting of Congress to January 3.

Section 5

Each House shall be the Judge of the Elections, Returns and Qualifications of its own Members, and a Majority of each shall constitute a Quorum to do Business; but a smaller Number may adjourn from day to day, and may be authorized to compel the Attendance of absent Members, in such Manner, and under such Penalties as each House may provide.

Each House may determine the Rules of its Proceedings, punish its Members for disorderly Behaviour, and, with the Concurrence of two thirds, expel a Member.

Each House shall keep a Journal of its Proceedings, and from time to time publish the same, excepting such Parts as may in their Judgment require Secrecy; and the Yeas and Nays of the Members of either House on any question shall, at the Desire of one fifth of those Present, be entered on the Journal.

Neither House, during the Session of Congress, shall, without the Consent of the other, adjourn for more than three days, nor to any other Place than that in which the two Houses shall be sitting.

The items in Article I, Section 5, giving each branch of the legislature control over its own proceedings, reflect a long-standing desire, dating back to the gradual evolution of the English parliament as a legislative body with powers independent of those of the king, to preserve the independence of the legislature from executive encroachment. This section of the Constitution also encourages openness in the publication and dissemination of the proceedings of Congress.

SECTION 6

The Senators and Representatives shall receive a Compensation for their Services, to be ascertained by Law, and paid out of the Treasury of the United States. They shall in all Cases, except Treason, Felony and Breach of the Peace, be privileged from Arrest during their Attendance at the Session of their respective Houses, and in going to and returning from the same; and for any Speech or Debate in either House, they shall not be questioned in any other Place.

No Senator or Representative shall, during the Time for which he was elected, be appointed to any civil Office under the Authority of the United States, which shall have been created, or the Emoluments whereof shall have been encreased during such time; and no Person holding any Office under the United States, shall be a Member of either House during his Continuance in Office.

🖙 The provision for paying salaries to members of Congress provoked some disagreement among the delegates, as at least some members of the Constitutional Convention thought that public servants should be virtuous and wealthy "gentlemen" capable of serving in office without the need to seek compensation.

The provision providing immunity from arrest except in cases of treason, felony, or breach of the peace was another attempt to ensure the independence of members of the legislature, and the provision prohibiting service in other public offices while serving in Congress marked a rejection of practices in the English parliament, where members of Parliament also served as ministers in the king's cabinet; more generally it reflected a desire to reinforce the principle of separation of powers.

Section 7

All bills for raising Revenue shall originate in the House of Representatives; but the Senate may propose or concur with Amendments as on other Bills.

Every Bill which shall have passed the House of Representatives and the Senate, shall, before it become a Law, be presented to the President of the United States: If he approve he shall sign it, but if not he shall return it, with his Objections to that House in which it shall have originated, who shall enter the Objections at large on their Journal, and proceed to reconsider it. If after such Reconsideration two thirds of that House shall agree to pass the Bill, it shall be sent, together with the Objections, to the other House, by which it shall likewise be reconsidered, and if approved by two thirds of that House, it shall become a Law. But in all such Cases the Votes of both Houses shall be determined by Yeas and Nays, and the Names of the Persons voting for and against the Bill shall be entered on the Journal of each House respectively. If any Bill shall not be returned by the President within ten Days (Sundays excepted) after it shall have been presented to him, the Same shall be a Law, in like Manner as if he had signed it, unless the Congress by their Adjournment prevent its Return, in which Case it shall not be a Law.

Every Order, Resolution, or Vote to which the Concurrence of the Senate and House of Representatives may be necessary (except on a question of Adjournment) shall be presented to the President of the United States; and before the Same shall take Effect, shall be approved by him, or being disapproved by him, shall be repassed by two thirds of the Senate and House of Representatives, according to the Rules and Limitations prescribed in the Case of a Bill.

☜ The power over the "purse" was considered the most important of the powers that any government could wield; indeed it was the British parliament's attempt to tax the colonies without their consent that precipitated the American Revolution. The decision to give the federal government the power to levy taxes—a power denied to the government under the Articles of Confederation—may well have been the most important one made by the delegates to the Convention. It is noteworthy, however, that they gave the "people's body," the House of Representatives, the power to originate revenue bills.

The next, lengthy portion of Article I, Section 7, is one of the hallmarks of the system of separation of powers and checks and balances. It spells out the process by which a legislative proposal must pass both houses of Congress and then receive the assent of the president before it can become law. It provides for a limited executive veto over congressional legislation but gives to the Congress the power, if it can muster a two-thirds majority, to override a presidential veto.

SECTION 8

The Congress shall have Power To lay and collect Taxes, Duties, Imposts and Excises, to pay the Debts and provide for the common Defence and general Welfare of the United States; but all Duties, Imposts and Excises shall be uniform throughout the United States:

To Borrow Money on the credit of the United States;

To regulate Commerce with foreign Nations, and among the several States, and with the Indian Tribes;

To establish an uniform Rule of Naturalization, and uniform Laws on the subject of Bankruptcies throughout the United States;

To coin Money, regulate the Value thereof, and of foreign Coin, and fix the Standard of Weights and Measures;

To provide for the Punishment of counterfeiting the Securities and current Coin of the United States;

To establish Post Offices and Post Roads;

To promote the Progress of Science and useful Arts, by securing for limited Times to Authors and Inventors the exclusive Right to their respective Writings and Discoveries;

To constitute Tribunals inferior to the supreme Court;

To define and punish Piracies and Felonies committed on the high Seas, and Offences against the Law of Nations;

To declare War, grant Letters of Marque and Reprisal, and make Rules concerning Captures on Land and Water;

To raise and support Armies, but no Appropriation of Money to that Use shall be for a longer Term than two Years;

To provide and maintain a Navy;

To make Rules for the Government and Regulation of the land and naval Forces;

To provide for calling forth the Militia to execute the Laws of the Union, suppress Insurrections and repel Invasions;

To provide for organizing, arming, and disciplining the Militia, and for governing such Part of them as may be employed in the Service of the United States, reserving to the States respectively, the Appointment of the Officers, and the Authority of training the Militia according to the discipline prescribed by Congress;

To exercise exclusive Legislation in all Cases whatsoever, over such District (not exceeding ten Miles square) as may, by Cession of particular States, and the Acceptance of Congress, become the Seat of the Government of the United States, and to exercise like Authority over all Places purchased by the Consent of the Legislature of the State in which the Same shall be, for the Erection of Forts, Magazines, Arsenals, dock-Yards, and other needful Buildings;—And

To make all Laws which shall be necessary and proper for carrying into Execution the foregoing Powers, and all other Powers vested by this Constitution in the Government of the United States, or in any Department or Officer thereof.

✏ Many Americans think of their Constitution as a document that protects the liberties of American citizens by defining those things that the federal government *cannot* do. This is the central concern of the first ten amendments to the Constitution, which today we call the Bill of Rights. But in fact, in many respects Article I, Section 8, constitutes the heart and soul of the U.S. Constitution. It specifically enumerates the powers that the federal government is permitted to exercise. The initial version of this article, as outlined in the Virginia Plan, gave an open-ended grant of power to the Congress, simply providing that Congress would have the power "to legislate in all cases to which the separate States are incompetent," but when the Committee of Detail produced a comprehensive first draft of a constitution in early August 1787, that general grant of power was replaced by the more specific enumeration of powers that appears in Article I, Section 8. Among the most important powers enumerated in Article I, Section 8, are:

1. As previously mentioned, the power to levy taxes—the ability of the government to provide for itself a permanent revenue with which to finance its operations—was the single most important power given to the new federal government. The broad purposes for which that power was granted—to "provide for the common Defence and general Welfare of the United States"—have been interpreted in widely different ways over the course of the nation's history, with the general trend leading toward an expansion of activity financed by the federal taxation power.

2. The "commerce power" has proven to be one of the most important and far-reaching provisions of the federal Constitution. Utilizing an ever-expanding definition of its power to regulate commerce "among the several States," the federal government has broadened the definition of "commerce" to include not only the shipment of goods across state lines but also many other forms of activity: the building of interstate roads; the power to regulate the business activities of corporations; and the power to pass environmental legislation, consumer-protection laws, and occupational-safety regulations.

3. Establishing post offices and post roads may seem mundane enterprises, but this provision of the Constitution, in conjunction with an expansive view of Congress's role in promoting the "general Welfare" and regulating commerce, marked the beginnings of the creation of a national infrastructure that would tie the thirteen previously independent and sovereign states into a single nation.

4. The clause relating to the promotion of science and useful arts gives to Congress the power to enact patent and copyright laws.

5. Clauses ten through sixteen of Article I, Section 8, deal with the war powers of Congress. If the "power over the purse" has long been considered to be the most important of a government's powers, the power over the "sword"—the ability not only to declare war but also to vote on appropriations for the financial support of war—has run a close second. Congress's power to declare war overlaps with the power of the president, as commander in chief of the nation's armed forces, to direct the actual conduct of war. In one sense, this overlap is part of the Constitution's system of separation of powers, but in another it has become a significant source of constitutional controversy in recent years. In numerous cases since the mid-twentieth century—in the Korean War, the Vietnam War, the First Gulf War, and most recently, the wars in Iraq and Afghanistan—the president has proceeded with the prosecution of the war without a formal congressional declaration of war.

6. Congress's power over the appropriation of money gives it a substantial say over how—or whether—a war should be fought, but it has only rarely denied funds for the support of an army or navy once a war is under way.

7. The seventeenth clause, giving to Congress the power to "exercise exclusive Legislation . . . over such District . . . as may . . . become the Seat of the Government," is the basis on which Congress created the District of Columbia, which is regarded not as a state but as a federal territory and the nation's capital.

8. The final provision of Article I, Section 8, has proven to be one of the most important—and controversial—provisions of the Constitution. By giving Congress the power to make all laws "necessary and proper" for carrying into effect the previously enumerated powers, the framers of the Constitution opened the door to a significant expansion of federal power. Within just a few years of the adoption of the Constitution, some of the most important figures of the revolutionary era found them-

selves in bitter disagreement on the meaning of the phrase "necessary and proper," with President Washington's secretary of the treasury, Alexander Hamilton, arguing for a broad construction of its meaning (for example, as "needful," "useful," or "conducive to") and Thomas Jefferson and James Madison arguing for a strict construction (for example, as "absolutely necessary"). This line of constitutional difference between "broad constructionists" and "strict constructionists" was a bitter source of contention in the period leading up to the Civil War and continues in somewhat diminished form between the respective proponents of a more limited or more active federal government even today.

SECTION 9

The Migration or Importation of such Persons as any of the States now existing shall think proper to admit, shall not be prohibited by the Congress prior to the Year one thousand eight hundred and eight, but a Tax or duty may be imposed on such Importation, not exceeding ten dollars for each Person.

The Privilege of the Writ of Habeas Corpus shall not be suspended, unless when in Cases of Rebellion or Invasion the public Safety may require it.

No Bill of Attainder or ex post facto Law shall be passed.

No Capitation, or other direct, Tax shall be laid, unless in Proportion to the Census or Enumeration herein before directed to be taken.

No Tax or Duty shall be laid on Articles exported from any State.

No Preference shall be given by any Regulation of Commerce or Revenue to the Ports of one State over those of another; nor shall Vessels bound to, or from, one State, be obliged to enter, clear, or pay Duties in another.

No Money shall be drawn from the Treasury, but in Consequence of Appropriations made by Law; and a regular Statement and Account of the Receipts and Expenditures of all public Money shall be published from time to time.

No Title of Nobility shall be granted by the United States: And no Person holding any Office of Profit or Trust under them, shall, without the Consent of the Congress, accept of any present, Emolument, Office, or Title, of any kind whatever, from any King, Prince or foreign State.

☞ Article I, Section 9, outlines those actions that the federal government *may not* take.

The most controversial of these prohibitions is contained in the very first item. The Convention delegates from South Carolina and Georgia, whose slave economies were still expanding, insisted that no legislation interfering with the African slave trade be permitted until at least twenty years after the adoption of the Constitution. The prohibition of any legislation affecting "the Migration or Importation of such Persons as any of the States now existing shall think proper to admit" was intended to ensure that protection. As in all instances in which the Constitution deals with the institution of slavery, neither the word "slave" nor "slavery" is explicitly mentioned in the text of the document. In 1808 the U.S. Congress enacted legislation abolishing the international slave trade, but during that twenty-year interval some two hundred thousand slaves were imported from Africa into the United States.

Many of the most important prohibitions to federal government action laid down in Article I, Section 9, were designed to protect fundamental liberties handed down to Americans through English common law. Perhaps the most important of these was the privilege of habeas corpus, the right of a prisoner to challenge his imprisonment in a court of law. On at least a few occasions American presidents have suspended this privilege while either suppressing rebellion or protecting the public safety. During the Civil War, President Abraham Lincoln held "disloyal persons" suspected of giving aid and comfort to the Confederate cause in prison without benefit of trial.

More recently, President George W. Bush, citing provisions of the Patriot Act as well as implied executive powers, sanctioned the holding of several hundred "enemy combatants" in the "war on terror."

The prohibition against bills of attainder, the issuing of edicts aimed at punishing individuals or groups of individuals without benefit of trial, and the ban on ex post facto laws—criminal laws aimed at punishing individuals for actions taken before the law itself was passed—were also rooted in traditions of English common law. The prohibition of taxes on exports was a purely political bargain between northern and southern states, and was designed to protect the interests of the South, whose agricultural exports formed an important part of its economy. The prohibition against direct taxes unless such taxes were levied precisely in proportion to the number of citizens in each of the states was another attempt to protect the institution of slavery from being taxed out of existence; this provision was subsequently changed by the passage of the Sixteenth Amendment, making possible the imposition of a federal income tax.

While it would be unthinkable today for our federal government to grant a title of nobility to any of its citizens, the provision in Article I, Section 9, prohibiting the granting of titles of nobility and placing additional restrictions on receiving a "present, Emolument, Office, or Title" from a foreign state reflected the strong commitment of the framers of the Constitution that their government should be a "republican" one, and not one that reflected the aristocratic ways of Europe.

Section 10

No State shall enter into any Treaty, Alliance, or Confederation; grant Letters of Marque and Reprisal; coin Money; emit Bills of Credit; make any Thing but gold and silver Coin a Tender in Payment of Debts; pass any Bill of Attainder, ex post facto Law, or Law impairing the Obligation of Contracts, or grant any Title of Nobility.

No State shall, without the Consent of the Congress, lay any Imposts or Duties on Imports or Exports, except what may be absolutely necessary for executing its inspection Laws: and the net Produce of all Duties and Imposts, laid by any State on Imports or Exports, shall be for the Use of the Treasury of the United States; and all such Laws shall be subject to the Revision and Controul of the Congress.

No State shall, without the Consent of Congress, lay any duty of Tonnage, keep Troops, or Ships of War in time of Peace, enter into any Agreement or Compact with another State, or with a foreign Power, or engage in War, unless actually invaded, or in such imminent Danger as will not admit of delay.

🖙 The provisions in Article I, Section 10, stipulate those things that the *state governments* are prohibited from doing. The most important of these are:

1. Individual states may not enter into separate treaties with foreign nations.

2. The governments of the states are bound by the same requirements as the federal government in the prohibition of bills of attainder, ex post facto laws, laws impairing obligations of contracts, and granting titles of nobility.

3. State governments may not issue currency for the purpose of paying debts unless that currency is in gold and silver. This provision came in reaction to the laxness of some state governments that issued depreciated or, in some cases, worthless currency during the period of the Revolution. This provision marked the beginning—but only the beginning—of the creation of a single national currency.

4. During the period of the Confederation, many states, eager to raise their own revenues, levied tariffs on goods entering their ports from other states. The new Constitution reserved the power of taxing imports to the federal government alone, preventing states from enacting their own tariffs.

5. Although the individual states were permitted to maintain their own militias for the maintenance of order within their boundaries, the Constitution prohibits states from maintaining either a standing army or a navy in time of peace; it also prohibits the states from entering into agreements with other states or foreign powers for military purposes.

ARTICLE II

Section 1

The executive Power shall be vested in a President of the United States of America. He shall hold his Office during the Term of four Years, and, together with the Vice President, chosen for the same Term, be elected, as follows:

Each State shall appoint, in such Manner as the Legislature thereof may direct, a Number of Electors, equal to the whole Number of Senators and Representatives to which the State may be entitled in the Congress: but no Senator or Representative, or Person holding an Office of Trust or Profit under the United States, shall be appointed an Elector.

The Electors shall meet in their respective States, and vote by Ballot for two Persons, of whom one at least shall not be an Inhabitant of the same State with themselves. And they shall make a List of all the Persons voted for, and of the Number of Votes for each; which List they shall sign and certify, and transmit sealed to the Seat of the Government of the United States, directed to the President of the Senate. The President of the Senate shall, in the Presence of the Senate and House of Representatives, open all the Certificates, and the Votes shall then be counted. The Person having the greatest Number of Votes shall be the President, if such Number be a Majority of the whole Number of Electors appointed; and if there be more than one who have such Majority, and have an equal Number of

Votes, then the House of Representatives shall immediately chuse by Ballot one of them for President; and if no Person have a Majority, then from the five highest on the List the said House shall in like Manner chuse the President. But in chusing the President, the Votes shall be taken by States, the Representation from each State having one Vote; a quorum for this Purpose shall consist of a Member or Members from two thirds of the States, and a Majority of all the States shall be necessary to a Choice. In every Case, after the Choice of the President, the Person having the greatest Number of Votes of the Electors shall be the Vice President. But if there should remain two or more who have equal Votes, the Senate shall chuse from them by Ballot the Vice President.

The Congress may determine the Time of chusing the Electors, and the Day on which they shall give their Votes; which Day shall be the same throughout the United States.

No person except a natural born Citizen, or a Citizen of the United States, at the time of the Adoption of this Constitution, shall be eligible to the Office of President; neither shall any Person be eligible to that Office who shall not have attained to the Age of thirty five Years, and been fourteen Years a Resident within the United States.

In Case of the Removal of the President from Office, or of his Death, Resignation, or Inability to discharge the Powers and Duties of the said Office, the Same shall devolve on the Vice President, and the Congress may by Law provide for the Case of Removal, Death, Resignation or Inability, both of the President and Vice President, declaring what Officer shall then act as President, and such Officer shall act accordingly, until the Disability be removed, or a President shall be elected.

The President shall, at stated Times, receive for his Services, a Compensation, which shall neither be increased nor diminished during the Period for which he shall have been elected, and he shall not receive within that Period any other Emolument from the United States, or any of them.

Before he enter on the Execution of his Office, he shall take the following Oath or Affirmation: "I do solemnly swear (or affirm) that I will faithfully execute the Office of President of the United States, and will to the best of my Ability, preserve, protect and defend the Constitution of the United States."

☞ The opening words of Article II, Section 1, are both remarkably simple and maddeningly vague: "The executive Power shall be vested in a President of the United States of America." While other sections of Article II provide some specificity on the nature and extent of presidential power, for the most part the language of Article II relating to executive power is far less specific than that of Article I defining congressional power.

Opinions about the length of the president's term varied widely, with proposals ranging from a minimum of two years to a term of "during good behavior"—or, effectively, for life. The delegates also disagreed about whether the president should be eligible for reelection. The decision on a four-year term seemed to satisfy most delegates and, by avoiding mentioning anything about the president's eligibility for reelection, the framers left the question of how many terms a president should serve up to the voters. George Washington's decision to serve only two terms in office set a precedent that lasted until the presidency of Franklin D. Roosevelt, who won election to the presidency four times, serving from 1933 until his death in 1945. In 1951 Congress passed, and the states ratified, the Twenty-second Amendment, limiting presidents to two terms.

The next part of Article II, Section 1, reflects the torment the Convention delegates experienced as they wrestled with the question of how to give the president sufficient power without giving him excessive power, as well as how to free him from excessive dependence on the legislature while at the same time assuring that he did not become, in their terms, an "elective monarch." While one would think that the best way to do this would be to have the president elected by and answerable to the people of the nation at large, the vast majority of delegates feared that the American people were simply too provincial—too ignorant of the merits of possible presidential candidates across a land as vast as that of the thirteen states of which America was then comprised—to make a wise choice. For that reason, for most of the Convention the delegates inclined toward election of the president by the Congress or, at least, by the more popular branch of Congress, the House of Representatives. But this method ran the risk of violating the principles of separation of powers by making the president unduly dependent upon the Congress for his election. For much of the summer of 1787, the delegates argued unproductively about various alternatives for electing the president, and finally, in the tortured language of Article II, Section 1, they called for the creation of an electoral college: a group of independent electors, selected in each of the states "in such Manner as the Legislature thereof may direct," who would then cast their ballots for a president and vice president.

Although initially designed as a decidedly elitist device by which only the most knowledgeable and distinguished men—those selected to be electors—would use their own independent judgment in casting their ballots for the president, by the election of Thomas Jefferson in 1800 the presidential electoral system had been entirely transformed by the unexpected invention of organized political parties. The newly created political party system functioned in a way that caused slates of presidential electors to be pledged in advance to vote for particular candidates, with the result being that American voters, whose numbers were expanding as the number of citizens eligible to vote expanded, were now casting their votes, not on the basis of the identity of the individual electors, but on the merits of the candidates themselves. The invention of political parties—a development occurring wholly outside America's constitutional system—fundamentally changed the way the Constitution operated, transforming it from a "republican" but elitist political system into a truly democratic one.

Americans have grumbled about the imperfections of the electoral college system from the days when it was first debated in the Constitutional Convention up to the present, but for the most part, it has managed to produce victors in the presidential contests whose legitimacy as duly elected chief executives has not been challenged. There have been exceptions: the election of John Quincy Adams, decided by the House of Representatives in 1824; the election of a "minority" Republican president, Abraham Lincoln, in 1860, which led to the secession of the Southern states; the disputed 1876 presidential election between Samuel Tilden and Rutherford B. Hayes, in the final days of Reconstruction; and the contested election of George W. Bush in 2000, ultimately decided by the Supreme Court. Each of these cases has provoked criticism of the electoral college system, but up to this point neither Congress nor the American people have moved to the obvious alternative: direct popular election of the president.

The decision to require that the president be a "natural born Citizen" of the United States was made in the Convention with little discussion and probably with little thought. Indeed, eight of the delegates to the Convention had themselves been born outside British North America (all were born in the British Isles and would in any case have been eligible to serve as president because they were citizens of the United States at the time of the adoption of the Constitution). In an age in which America's economy, culture, and politics are increasingly shaped by recent immigrants, this particular constitutional provision seems a good candidate for amendment.

This provision defines the vice president's most important duty: to succeed the president in case of his death, disability, or removal from office. The framers left the line of succession in the event of the vice president's death, disability, resignation, or removal up to Congress. The Twenty-fifth Amendment, adopted in 1967, provided a means by which a president could select, with the confirmation of a majority of members of Congress, another vice president.

Although Congress is given responsibility for setting the president's salary, it may not increase or decrease his salary during his term of service, a provision designed to render the president independent of the Congress's will.

The presidential oath is a remarkably simple one, wholly appropriate to a republican society. In taking the oath of office for the first time on April 30, 1789, George Washington added the words "So help me, God" to his oath, a tradition that has been continued by nearly every subsequent president.

Section 2

The President shall be Commander in Chief of the Army and Navy of the United States, and of the Militia of the several States, when called into the actual Service of the United States; he may require the Opinion, in writing, of the principal Officer in each of the executive Departments, upon any Subject relating to the Duties of their respective Offices, and he shall have Power to grant Reprieves and Pardons for Offences against the United States, except in Cases of Impeachment.

He shall have Power, by and with the Advice and Consent of the Senate, to make Treaties, provided two thirds of the Senators present concur; and he shall nominate, and by and with the Advice and Consent of the Senate, shall appoint Ambassadors, other public Ministers and Consuls, Judges of the supreme Court, and all other Officers of the United States, whose Appointments are not herein otherwise provided for, and which shall be established by Law: but the Congress may by Law vest the Appointment of such inferior Officers, as they think proper, in the President alone, in the Courts of Law, or in the Heads of Departments.

The President shall have Power to fill up all Vacancies that may happen during the Recess of the Senate, by granting Commissions which shall expire at the End of their next Session.

Article II, Section 2, is principally concerned with outlining the powers of the president, but given the enormous power of the modern presidency, it seems remarkably short and vague in its prescriptions. Certainly, the most important—and controversial—of those powers has devolved from the president's role as commander in chief of the army and navy of the United States and of the militias of the several states. That role, which has given the president enormous power to "make war," has sometimes come in conflict with the power of Congress to "declare war" as well as with Congress's power to control the financial appropriations necessary to make fighting a war possible.

By the terms of Article II, Section 2, the president has the primary role in entering into treaties with other nations, although it reserves to the Senate the right to approve any treaty before it assumes the force of law.

The president has the power, with the advice and consent of the Senate, to appoint ambassadors, ministers, justices of the Supreme Court, and "all other Officers of the United States." In recent decades, as the Supreme Court has become a more powerful and assertive branch of the federal government, members of the Senate have responded by asserting more vigorously *their* right to advise and consent with respect to the appointment of justices of the Court.

The president's use of the power to appoint "all other Officers of the United States" has increased in direct proportion to the growing power of the federal government and of the executive branch in particular. Although the Founding Fathers no doubt assumed that the president would appoint members of a presidential "cabinet," they would perhaps have been surprised at the growth in the size and scope of the bureaucracy serving each of the cabinet departments. The president's cabinet has expanded from four members in President Washington's day (the secretaries of treasury, war, and state and the attorney general) to fifteen (not including the vice president) today.

Section 3

He shall from time to time give to the Congress Information of the State of the Union, and recommend to their Consideration such Measures as he shall judge necessary and expedient; he may, on extraordinary Occasions, convene both Houses, or either of them, and in Case of Disagreement between them, with Respect to the Time of Adjournment, he may adjourn them to such Time as he shall think proper; he shall receive Ambassadors and other public Ministers; he shall take Care that the Laws be faithfully executed, and shall Commission all the Officers of the United States.

☞ Presidents Washington and Adams addressed the Congress directly on the "State of the Union," but from 1801 to 1909 the president merely sent the Congress written messages. Beginning in 1913, and continuing to the present day, the formal State of the Union address to Congress, given at the beginning of each year, has become an important national ritual. Some presidents, including President Barack Obama, have convened both houses of Congress on other "extraordinary Occasions," to address them on subjects that they have considered important.

Section 4

The President, Vice President and all civil Officers of the United States, shall be removed from Office on Impeachment for, and Conviction of, Treason, Bribery, or other high Crimes and Misdemeanors.

☞ This is another one of the provisions of Article II that is remarkably simple and maddeningly vague. The framers of the Constitution all agreed that a president should be removed from office if he committed treason, bribery, or other "high Crimes," but most of them also believed that the president might be removed if he were found culpable of "malfeasance in office" (a term used in one of the earlier drafts of the Constitution). On the other hand, most of the framers agreed that it would be improper for Congress to remove a president simply because a majority of members of Congress might disagree with him, and since "malfeasance" was a term with a meaning that might vary in the eye of the beholder, they substituted the term "Misdemeanors" for "malfeasance." It was a term that left no one wholly satisfied, and it has caused considerable confusion in those rare cases (during the presidencies of Andrew Johnson, Richard Nixon, and William Jefferson Clinton) in which impeachment proceedings against a president have been initiated.

ARTICLE III
SECTION 1

The judicial Power of the United States shall be vested in one supreme Court, and in such inferior Courts as the Congress may from time to time ordain and establish. The Judges, both of the supreme and inferior Courts, shall hold their Offices during good Behaviour, and shall, at stated Times, receive for their Services a Compensation which shall not be diminished during their Continuance in Office.

✒ Just as the framers of the Constitution considered the Congress to be the most vital branch of the new government and therefore dealt with that branch in the very first article of the Constitution, so too was the placement of the judicial branch in Article III of the Constitution a reflection of their view of the relative importance of that branch. The brevity and vagueness of the language in Article III are similarly a reflection of their relative lack of concern about the judicial branch as well as of their uncertainty about its function in the new federal union.

Article III, Section 1, stipulates that there would be one "supreme" court in the nation but is vague about the number and extent of the "inferior" courts. The provision that all federal judges should hold their offices during "good Behaviour" was intended to protect the independence of the judiciary and reinforce the separation of powers among the three branches of the new government.

Section 2

The judicial Power shall extend to all Cases, in Law and Equity, arising under this Constitution, the Laws of the United States, and Treaties made, or which shall be made, under their Authority; to all Cases affecting Ambassadors, other public Ministers and Consuls; to all Cases of admiralty and maritime Jurisdiction; to Controversies to which the United States shall be a Party; to Controversies between two or more States; between a State and Citizens of another State; between Citizens of different States; between Citizens of the same State claiming Lands under Grants of different States; and between a State, or the Citizens thereof, and foreign States, Citizens or Subjects.

In all Cases affecting Ambassadors, other public Ministers and Consuls, and those in which a State shall be Party, the supreme Court shall have original Jurisdiction. In all the other Cases before mentioned, the supreme Court shall have appellate Jurisdiction, both as to Law and Fact, with such Exceptions, and under such Regulations as the Congress shall make.

The Trial of all Crimes, except in Cases of Impeachment, shall be by Jury; and such Trial shall be held in the State where the said Crimes shall have been committed; but when not committed within any State, the Trial shall be at such Place or Places as the Congress may by Law have directed.

☞ Article III, Section 2, defines the jurisdiction and mode of procedure of the federal courts. The key phrase is "to all Cases, in Law and Equity, arising under this Constitution." In other words, the jurisdiction of the federal courts extends to those areas in which the United States government itself has jurisdiction. That jurisdiction, vaguely defined in 1787, has steadily increased over the more than two centuries in which the Constitution has been in operation.

Although Article III, Section 2, makes no mention of a power of judicial review (the power of the Supreme Court or any other federal court to pass judgment on whether a federal or state law violates the terms of the Constitution), many, if not most, of the delegates to the Convention probably assumed that the federal courts would exercise at least some limited form of that power. In 1803, in the case of *Marbury v. Madison*, the Supreme Court, in an opinion written by its chief justice, John Marshall, enunciated a limited power of judicial review.

Section 3

Treason against the United States, shall consist only in levying War against them, or in adhering to their Enemies, giving them Aid and Comfort. No Person shall be convicted of Treason unless on the Testimony of two Witnesses to the same overt Act, or on Confession in open Court.

The Congress shall have power to declare the Punishment of Treason, but no Attainder of Treason shall work Corruption of Blood, or Forfeiture except during the Life of the Person attainted.

☞ Article III, Section 3, is the only instance in which the U.S. Constitution defines a specific crime, that of treason. Treason is defined either as levying war against the United States or as giving "Aid and Comfort" to the enemies of the United States. The "Aid and Comfort" clause expands the definition of treason beyond physical acts of violence—e.g., to the passing on of state secrets to another nation—but the Constitution also lays down specific legal procedures by which people accused of treason might be convicted of such an act. The Constitution further limits the punishment of treason to the person actually committing the act, not to family members or close associates.

In 1807, in the treason trial of Aaron Burr, for his role in an alleged plan to lead parts of the Louisiana territory in a secessionist movement from the United States, Chief Justice John Marshall laid down further limitations on the definition of treason, establishing the doctrine of "constructive treason," meaning that the mere planning of an act that might be considered treasonous was not sufficient grounds for conviction; in order to be convicted of treason one actually had to commit, or at least be in the process of committing, the act. Moreover, the act of simply speaking, however stridently, in a manner that some might believe to be giving aid and comfort to the enemy was given further protection by the free speech guarantees of the First Amendment.

ARTICLE IV

SECTION 1

Full Faith and Credit shall be given in each State to the public Acts, Records, and judicial Proceedings of every other State. And the Congress may by general Laws prescribe the Manner in which such Acts, Records and Proceedings shall be proved, and the Effect thereof.

The first section of Article IV stipulates that the laws of one state must be given "full Faith and Credit" (i.e., be recognized as legitimate) in another state. This provision was an important step in creating a uniform standard of law and of rights in the nation. For example, if the state of Massachusetts recognizes the marriage of a gay couple as legally valid, then other states, even if they do not have laws permitting the marriage of a gay couple, must recognize that marriage as valid.

SECTION 2

The Citizens of each State shall be entitled to all Privileges and Immunities of Citizens in the several States.

A Person charged in any State with Treason, Felony, or other Crime, who shall flee from Justice, and be found in another State, shall on Demand of the executive Authority of the State from which he fled, be delivered up, to be removed to the State having Jurisdiction of the Crime.

No Person held to Service or Labour in one State, under the Laws thereof, escaping into another, shall, in Consequence of any Law or Regulation therein, be discharged from such Service or Labour, but shall be delivered up on Claim of the Party to whom such Service or Labour may be due.

☞ The first provision of Article IV, Section 2, is a cornerstone of a common standard for equal protection under the law for all American citizens. It gives to citizens of every state all the legal protections enjoyed by citizens of other states if they should be residing in or traveling through one of those other states. This means, for example, that New Jersey cannot give citizens of that state one set of rights while at the same time denying a citizen of New York living or working in New Jersey any of those same rights. Therefore New Jersey cannot impose higher taxes on New Yorkers working in New Jersey than it imposes on its own residents.

The other side of the "privileges and immunity" clause is that which requires states to respect the laws of other states aimed at punishing persons charged with "Treason, Felony, or other Crime" by extraditing (delivering up) such persons to the state having jurisdiction over the crime.

The final part of Article IV, Section 2, may well be the most reprehensible provision in the original U.S. Constitution. It requires that the governments and citizens of every state in the union deliver up all persons "held to Service or Labour in one State, under the Laws thereof, escaping into another." Although nowhere mentioned, those persons "held to Service or Labour" were slaves, and by requiring that citizens and states where slavery was not permitted cooperate with citizens and governments in slave-owning states in the return of their slaves, it made all Americans actively complicit in protecting the institution of slavery. This provision was rendered null and void by the passage of the Thirteenth Amendment, which abolished slavery.

Section 3

New States may be admitted by the Congress into this Union; but no new State shall be formed or erected within the Jurisdiction of any other State; nor any State be formed by the Junction of two or more States, or Parts of States, without the Consent of the Legislatures of the States concerned as well as of the Congress.

The Congress shall have Power to dispose of and make all needful Rules and Regulations respecting the Territory or other Property belonging to the United States; and nothing in this Constitution shall be so construed as to Prejudice any Claims of the United States, or of any particular State.

In 1787 the framers of the Constitution were mindful that, in addition to the thirteen original states, America consisted of a vast territory between the borders of those states and the Mississippi River. Article IV, Section 3, grants to Congress the authority to admit new states into the union on an equal basis with existing states. However, individual states are not permitted either to divide themselves into separate states (for example, California, by the terms of the Constitution, is not permitted to divide itself into two states; e.g., Northern California and Southern California), nor is it possible for two or more states (for example, Rhode Island and Connecticut) to combine their territories into a single state without the consent both of the legislatures of the states involved and of Congress.

The second part of Article IV, Section 3, gives to Congress considerable leeway as to what it might do in territories that have not achieved the status of a state within the federal union. Under this provision, Congress was able to grant independence to the Philippines, which was once a territory of the United States, and to extend certain rights (for example, the right of U.S. citizenship, although not the right to vote in presidential elections) to territories like Puerto Rico. This congressional jurisdiction also extends to the District of Columbia, which, though its citizens enjoy most of the rights of citizens of the fifty American states, is not at present fully represented in Congress.

SECTION 4

The United States shall guarantee to every State in this Union a Republican Form of Government, and shall protect each of them against Invasion; and on Application of the Legislature, or of the Executive (when the Legislature cannot be convened), against domestic Violence.

🖐 If there is a single idea expressed in Section 4 of Article IV on which all the framers of the Constitution agreed, it was that America should have a republican form of government, both in the polities of the individual states and in the new federal structure that they were creating. However, there were probably as many variations in the meaning of the word "republican" as there were delegates, ranging from those who wanted a democratic government directly responsive to the people to those who wished for a more elitist government, responsible to—but somewhat removed from—the people at large. The two core elements of republicanism on which all delegates could agree were that the government should be, either directly or indirectly, "representative" in character and that its officeholders should not base their claims to public office on hereditary privilege.

The second item in this section of Article IV was a direct response to one of the events that precipitated the calling of a Constitutional Convention: an armed uprising of farmers in western Massachusetts, known as Shays' Rebellion. The Constitution promises states protection against both internal uprisings and invasions from abroad but at the same time assures the states that the government will not interfere in their defense unless asked to do so by officials in the states themselves.

ARTICLE V

The Congress, whenever two thirds of both Houses shall deem it necessary, shall propose Amendments to this Constitution, or, on the Application of the Legislatures of two thirds of the several States, shall call a Convention for proposing Amendments, which, in either Case, shall be valid to all Intents and Purposes, as Part of this Constitution, when ratified by the Legislatures of three fourths of the several States, or by Conventions in three fourths thereof, as the one or the other Mode of Ratification may be proposed by the Congress; Provided that no Amendment which may be made prior to the Year one thousand eight hundred and eight shall in any Manner affect the first and fourth Clauses in the Ninth Section of the first Article; and that no State, without its Consent, shall be deprived of its equal Suffrage in the Senate.

☞ The Constitutional Convention of 1787 was called together to amend the Articles of Confederation, the existing frame of government that sought to create a union among the thirteen independent and sovereign states. By the terms of the Articles of Confederation, unanimous approval of all of the state legislatures was required to amend any major feature of that frame of government. That provision proved to be fatally flawed, for it soon became apparent that it was impossible to attain unanimity on any matter of consequence. The delegates to the Constitutional Convention, having already gone forward not merely with amendments to the Articles of Confederation but rather with a decision to scrap the Articles altogether and create a vastly strengthened central government, felt no compunctions about changing the formula for amendment, providing two different routes by which the new Constitution could be amended. Amendments can be proposed either by a two-thirds vote of both houses of Congress or when two-thirds of the legislatures of the states agree on calling a national convention for the purpose of proposing amendments. Amendments proposed by either method must, in order to become part of the Constitution, receive the approval of three-quarters of the state legislatures or be approved by specially called conventions in at least three-quarters of the states. Most of the amendments to the Constitution have been first proposed by Congress and then adopted by three-quarters of the state legislatures, although the Twenty-first Amendment, repealing prohibition, was adopted by conventions in three-quarters of the states.

The amendment process is an arduous one, and for that reason, relatively few amendments have been passed during the more than two hundred years since the Constitution was adopted, making it one of the most concise written constitutions in the world. Ten of the amendments—those that we consider to be part of the Bill of Rights—were proposed by the First Congress of the United States and quickly adopted by the necessary number of states within a few years after the new government commenced operation. During the whole of the nineteenth century, only five amendments were adopted, three of them coming in the immediate aftermath of the Civil War and dealing with the rights of newly freed slaves. Twelve amendments were passed in the twentieth century.

Among the most important were those authorizing a federal income tax, giving women a constitutional right to vote, providing for direct election of United States Senators, and guaranteeing all American citizens eighteen years or older the right to vote.

Article V also mentions three specific instances in which the Constitution is not subject to amendment: the provision prohibiting legislation affecting the international slave trade until 1808, the prohibition against direct taxation unless apportioned according to population, and the provision guaranteeing each state equal representation in the United States Senate.

ARTICLE VI

All Debts contracted and Engagements entered into, before the Adoption of this Constitution, shall be as valid against the United States under this Constitution, as under the Confederation.

This Constitution, and the Laws of the United States which shall be made in Pursuance thereof; and all Treaties made, or which shall be made, under the Authority of the United States, shall be the supreme Law of the Land; and the Judges in every State shall be bound thereby, any Thing in the Constitution or Laws of any State to the Contrary notwithstanding.

The Senators and Representatives before mentioned, and the Members of the several State Legislatures, and all executive and judicial Officers, both of the United States and of the several States, shall be bound by Oath or Affirmation, to support this Constitution; but no religious Test shall ever be required as a Qualification to any Office or public Trust under the United States.

☞ At the time the Constitution was created, the Continental government, the individual governments of the states, and many private citizens had all accumulated substantial debt obligations. The first item in Article VI was designed to ensure the sanctity of those debt obligations.

Article VI contains the so-called federal supremacy clause, the assertion that in cases of conflict between a state law and a federal law, the federal law takes precedence. Over the course of the nation's history, there have been hundreds of cases where the overlapping jurisdictions of the states and the federal government (for example, in matters relating to the regulation of commerce, industry, or environmental policy) have led to lawsuits. In general, although not uniformly, the federal supremacy clause has worked to incline courts to side with the federal government.

The final item in Article VI requires officials in both the state and federal governments to uphold the Constitution of the United States. This item is also the only place in the body of the Constitution where religion is explicitly mentioned. It is notable that this sole mention of religion reinforces the principle of separation of church and state, decreeing that there shall be no religious test for holding public office.

ARTICLE VII

The Ratification of the Conventions of nine States, shall be sufficient for the Establishment of this Constitution between the States so ratifying the Same.

Having exceeded their instructions from the Continental Congress by scrapping the Articles of Confederation and drafting a wholly new frame of government, the framers of the Constitution also ignored the provision in the Articles of Confederation requiring unanimous approval of the state legislatures in order to amend that frame of government. The decision to allow the Constitution to go into operation after the approval of only nine of the thirteen states made it much easier to secure ratification of the document.

Moreover, the device of submitting the document for consideration by specially called state conventions rather than by state legislatures avoided some of the natural tendencies of state legislators to protect their powers and interests. Most important though, the use of conventions, elected directly by the people of the states and called together solely for the purpose of considering the new plan of union, signified that the proposed new government was intended to be a government founded on "We the People of the United States," rather than merely on "we the states."

Done in Convention by the Unanimous Consent of the States present the Seventeenth Day of September in the Year of our Lord one thousand seven hundred and Eighty seven and of the Independence of the United States of America the Twelfth. In Witness whereof We have hereunto subscribed our Names.

Attest William Jackson, Secretary

Go. Washington, President and deputy from Virginia

🖙 There were forty-one delegates present in the Assembly Room of the Pennsylvania State House on September 17, 1787. Thirty-eight of the delegates in the room signed the completed Constitution, with George Mason and Edmund Randolph of Virginia and Elbridge Gerry of Massachusetts refusing to add their assent. A forty-second delegate, John Dickinson of Delaware, had been suffering from debilitating headaches and went home a few days earlier, but he asked his Delaware colleague George Read to sign the document for him, bringing the total number of signatories to thirty-nine.

DELAWARE
Geo. Read
Gunning Bedford Jr.
John Dickinson
Richard Bassett
Jaco. Broom

MARYLAND
James McHenry
Dan of St. Thos. Jenifer
Danl. Carroll

VIRGINIA
John Blair
James Madison Jr.

NORTH CAROLINA
Wm. Blount
Richd. Dobbs Spaight
Hu Williamson

SOUTH CAROLINA
J. Rutledge
Charles Cotesworth Pinckney
Charles Pinckney
Pierce Butler

GEORGIA
William Few
Abr. Baldwin

NEW HAMPSHIRE
John Langdon
Nicholas Gilman

MASSACHUSETTS
Nathaniel Gorham
Rufus King

CONNECTICUT
Wm. Saml. Johnson
Roger Sherman

NEW YORK
Alexander Hamilton

NEW JERSEY
Wil. Livingston
David Brearley
Wm. Paterson
Jona. Dayton

PENNSYLVANIA
B. Franklin
Thomas Mifflin
Robt. Morris
Geo. Clymer
Thos. FitzSimons
Jared Ingersoll
James Wilson
Gouv. Morris

AMENDMENTS TO THE CONSTITUTION

The framers of the original Constitution assumed that it was not necessary to include a "bill of rights" in their proposed plan for the union. The ostensible reason for the omission was that most of the state constitutions already possessed bills of rights, and therefore the inclusion of a bill of rights in the federal Constitution would be redundant. Another, more compelling reason may have been that when the idea of a bill of rights was raised in early September by Virginia delegate George Mason, the members of the Convention, tired and desperate to return home, feared that a debate on the subject might extend their stay in Philadelphia by many weeks, if not months.

The omission of a bill of rights proved to be both a tactical and strategic error. When the Constitution was submitted to the states for ratification, many of the critics of the Constitution pointed to the absence of a bill of rights as a fatal flaw in the document. As a consequence, the supporters of the Constitution, who called themselves Federalists, came forward with a promise to make the drafting of a bill of rights the first item of business when the new Congress convened after the ratification of the Constitution. On September 25, 1789, Congress presented to the states twelve amendments, ten of which received the necessary approval of three-quarters of the states on December 15, 1791. It is those ten amendments that are commonly referred to as the Bill of Rights. One of the two amendments not approved, dealing with congressional representation, has not proved of any significance in the operation of the Constitution. The other, dealing with congressional salaries, was eventually incorporated into the Twenty-seventh Amendment.

AMENDMENT I (1791)

Congress shall make no law respecting an establishment of religion, or prohibiting the free exercise thereof; or abridging the freedom of speech, or of the press; or the right of the people peaceably to assemble, and to petition the Government for a redress of grievances.

The First Amendment is remarkably brief considering the breadth of protection that it has provided. The section of the amendment prohibiting Congress from making any law "respecting an establishment of religion" is a cornerstone of the American notion of separation of church and state, and the guarantee of "free exercise" of religion has proven a powerful means by which people have been allowed to express their religious beliefs without fear of government reprisal. Similarly, the guarantees of freedom of speech, of the press, and of the "right of the people peaceably to assemble," as well as the right to petition their government (and by implication to protest the actions of that government) are at the heart of the American constitutional definition of liberty.

Those freedoms have, however, been subject to some restrictions. Until the early twentieth century, the First Amendment applied only to the actions of the federal government; state governments were free to pass their own laws contravening some of the provisions of the First Amendment. For example, the state of Massachusetts continued to accord the Congregational Church special privileges and did not move to explicitly separate church and state until 1833. Moreover, throughout the nineteenth century, and sometimes into the twentieth, state governments have enacted laws placing restrictions on speech, freedom of the press, and on certain forms of public assembly. It was only in the twentieth century, through application of the "incorporation doctrine," that the Fourteenth Amendment's guarantee that states must not "abridge the privileges or immunities of citizens of the United States," nor deny citizens "equal protection of the laws," began to obligate state governments to guarantee their residents the same freedoms as those articulated in the First Amendment.

The precise extent of the guarantees of the First Amendment continues to be a subject of contention. Oliver Wendell Holmes, in a Supreme Court opinion in *Schenck v. United States* (1919), made the commonsense argument that the guarantees of free speech do not extend to the right to shout "fire in a theatre and causing a panic" when no such danger actually exists. Governments have often asserted the right to regulate public assemblies and protests in order to ensure public safety.

Similarly, the "wall of separation" between church and state is not impenetrable. The United States Congress continues to employ a chaplain, and the word of God is frequently invoked at many official government gatherings. The federal courts are frequently presented with cases in which litigants claim that public displays of religious belief (e.g., the displaying of a Nativity scene in a public square at Christmastime) violate the principle of separation of church and state. Thus far there is no clear resolution of where the boundary between a religious and a civic display lies.

AMENDMENT II (1791)

A well regulated Militia, being necessary to the security of a free State, the right of the people to keep and bear Arms, shall not be infringed.

☞ The Second Amendment contains two parts: a preface, which states that a "well regulated Militia" (meaning a citizens' army authorized by the state) is a necessary and desirable thing, and the operative section of the amendment, which asserts the right of the people to keep and bear arms. Constitutional scholars have argued vociferously about whether the comma separating those two parts signifies that the right to keep and bear arms without state interference is confined to the use of such arms in conjunction with one's duties as part of a government-sanctioned militia or army, or whether there is an individual right to keep and bear arms under any circumstances. The most recent ruling of the Supreme Court (*District of Columbia v. Heller*, 2008) suggests that the Second Amendment does guarantee an individual, as well as a collective, right to bear arms, but the Court has also conceded that there are some instances (e.g., regulating the sale of assault weapons) in which local, state, and federal governments do have the right to regulate the sale and use of arms. Like many aspects of the Constitution, the meaning of the Second Amendment is subject to varying interpretations.

AMENDMENT III (1791)

No Soldier shall, in time of peace be quartered in any house, without the consent of the Owner, nor in time of war, but in a manner to be prescribed by law.

⚓ This amendment, which has lost much of its immediacy over the course of time, was considered of pressing importance by the members of the First Congress, who drafted it because attempts to force Americans to provide lodgings for British troops (whom they considered to be hostile occupiers of their land) during the years leading to the Revolution were an important cause of that revolution. The amendment does, "in a manner to be prescribed by law," allow the government to use private homes to provide lodging for its own soldiers in time of war. More generally, the Third Amendment has—along with the Fourth, Fifth, and Ninth Amendments—been interpreted to imply another right not explicitly mentioned in the Constitution: the right of privacy.

AMENDMENT IV (1791)

The right of the people to be secure in their persons, houses, papers, and effects, against unreasonable searches and seizures, shall not be violated, and no Warrants shall issue, but upon probable cause, supported by Oath or affirmation, and particularly describing the place to be searched, and the persons or things to be seized.

☞ The guarantees against "unreasonable searches and seizures" of persons, houses, and property, and the insistence that any such searches be based on "probable cause" and accompanied by search warrants, were another product of Americans' experience during the Revolution, when British customs officers and soldiers carried out blanket searches and seizures without proper warrants. In recent years, through use of the incorporation doctrine, the Fourth Amendment has been interpreted to mean that police officers at all levels of government must demonstrate probable cause before stopping and searching anyone whom they might suspect of a crime. The precise definition of "probable cause" has been much debated, and in many cases police officers are forced to make difficult judgments about whether they should detain an individual and search his or her possessions.

In an age in which advances in technology have offered the government new ways to gather evidence of a possible crime—e.g., wiretapping and other means of sophisticated electronic surveillance—the federal courts have been presented with new dilemmas about how to interpret the provisions of the Fourth Amendment. Enactment of the Patriot Act in the aftermath of the 9/11 attacks in 2001 has significantly expanded the government's ability to carry out such surveillance.

AMENDMENT V (1791)

No person shall be held to answer for a capital, or otherwise infamous crime, unless on a presentment or indictment of a Grand Jury, except in cases arising in the land or naval forces, or in the Militia, when in actual service in time of War or public danger; nor shall any person be subject for the same offence to be twice put in jeopardy of life or limb; nor shall be compelled in any criminal case to be a witness against himself, nor be deprived of life, liberty, or property, without due process of law; nor shall private property be taken for public use, without just compensation.

Reflecting long-standing traditions of English common law, as well as the American perception that the British had violated those traditions in the years leading up to the American Revolution, the Fifth Amendment requires that people charged with capital crimes (i.e., a serious crime that falls under the jurisdiction of the federal courts) be first presented before a grand jury—a group of ordinary citizens drawn from the general population. Those serving in the military are not afforded that protection; they are to be tried in military courts, which set their own rules of judicial procedure.

Although indictment by a grand jury is standard practice in important civil and criminal proceedings at the federal level, many states have not used this mechanism for securing indictments of accused criminals, believing that grand juries are unnecessarily costly and time-consuming. Although many of the provisions of the Bill of Rights have been applied to the actions of state governments through the incorporation doctrine of the Fourteenth Amendment, the Supreme Court has not asserted that states are bound to conform to this particular provision of the Fifth Amendment.

The provision of the Fifth Amendment preventing double jeopardy stipulates that individuals cannot be tried for the same crime more than once. If a defendant is acquitted of a crime, the government does not have the right to prosecute that individual again, and if a defendant is convicted, the government may not impose multiple punishments for the same crime.

The phrase "taking the Fifth" refers to the provision of the Fifth Amendment ensuring the right against self-incrimination: the right to refuse to answer questions in court that might lead either to indictment or punishment for an alleged crime. Finally, the Fifth Amendment contains a very open-ended guarantee, echoing the words of the preamble of the Declaration of Independence, that no person can be deprived of the fundamental rights of life, liberty, or property without due process of law.

The concern for protection of property is further emphasized in the prohibition of the taking of private property for public use "without just compensation." In fact, federal and state governments have often taken control of private property (for example, for the purposes of building a highway or some other necessary public work) by using the doctrine of "eminent domain." In those cases, the owners are compensated for the value of their property, although in many cases not without significant litigation.

AMENDMENT VI (1791)

In all criminal prosecutions, the accused shall enjoy the right to a speedy and public trial, by an impartial jury of the State and district wherein the crime shall have been committed, which district shall have been previously ascertained by law, and to be informed of the nature and cause of the accusation; to be confronted with the witnesses against him; to have compulsory process for obtaining witnesses in his favor, and to have the Assistance of Counsel for his defence.

☞ The Sixth Amendment is appropriately considered the centerpiece of the American criminal justice system. In addition to guaranteeing all criminal defendants a trial by jury, it provides an outline of the basic procedures to be followed in such trials. The trial shall be a speedy one, which is to say that accused criminals cannot be imprisoned for lengthy periods of time before receiving a trial. The trial must be public. The framers of the Sixth Amendment specifically rejected the format of English Star Chamber proceedings; that is, proceedings held in private, away from scrutiny by the public. The juries in criminal trials should, in normal instances, be drawn from ordinary citizens who are resident in the state and region where the crime was committed (although in unusual cases, if the crime is of such a sensational nature that it might prove impossible to impanel an *impartial* jury, the trial might be held in a jurisdiction other than the one in which the crime was committed).

The Sixth Amendment also guarantees to the accused the right to be confronted with the nature of the charges brought against him; the right to confront, either directly or through an attorney, the witnesses against him; and the right to present witnesses in his defense. Finally, criminal defendants are entitled to "Assistance of Counsel"; that is, a competent attorney to assist them in their defense. These basic guarantees have been elaborated in countless court cases in the more than two hundred years since the amendment was ratified and, through the incorporation doctrine, have become the standard procedure for criminal trials in states and other localities as well as in federal courts.

AMENDMENT VII (1791)

In Suits at common law, where the value in controversy shall exceed twenty dollars, the right of trial by jury shall be preserved, and no fact tried by a jury, shall be otherwise re-examined in any Court of the United States, than according to the rules of the common law.

☞ The Seventh Amendment provides guarantees similar to those of the Sixth with respect to civil suits, although it does limit the right of trial by jury to suits in which there are substantial sums of money involved. The terms and extent of the application of this amendment have been worked out through myriad court cases involving plaintiffs (the person bringing the suit) and defendants (the person being sued). For example, while the standard for conviction in a criminal trial is a jury's unanimous verdict that the accused criminal is guilty "beyond a reasonable doubt," a jury in a civil case may award damages to a plaintiff if a majority of jurors find a "preponderance of evidence" on his or her behalf. The incorporation doctrine has not been applied to this amendment and, for the present, civil suits tried in state and local courts may follow different procedures from those outlined in the Seventh Amendment.

AMENDMENT VIII (1791)

Excessive bail shall not be required, nor excessive fines imposed, nor cruel and unusual punishments inflicted.

👉 The prohibition against excessive bail (a sum of money put up to gain release from prison while awaiting a trial and returned if and when the accused appears for trial) is a reflection of the belief that an accused criminal is "presumed innocent until found guilty." The definition of "excessive bail" is a subjective one, but the intent of the amendment is to demand a sum of money sufficient to guarantee that the accused does show up for the trial, but not so high as to make it impossible for the accused to gain release.

The prohibition of "excessive fines" is intended to assure that "the punishment fits the crime." It is closely connected in its rationale with the final section of the amendment, the guarantee against "cruel and unusual punishments." Again drawing on English common law traditions, Americans were seeking to move away from ancient practices of gruesome punishments for relatively minor offenses. The definition of "cruel and unusual punishments" has often proven a point of contention. Currently, opponents of the death penalty argue that that punishment qualifies as cruel and unusual. Except for a period during the 1970s, the Supreme Court has not agreed, and both state governments and the federal government are free to permit executions if they desire (at present, thirty-five of the fifty states have laws permitting death penalties in some cases—usually, but not exclusively, murder cases).

AMENDMENT IX (1791)

The enumeration in the Constitution, of certain rights, shall not be construed to deny or disparage others retained by the people.

✒ One of the reasons given for the framers' omission of a Bill of Rights from the original Constitution was their fear that if they unintentionally failed to mention some fundamental rights in such a listing, those rights might go unprotected. That concern caused many of the delegates to fear that any debate over a bill of rights might drag on for weeks or months, as they sought to cover every conceivable right. The Ninth Amendment makes it clear that the list of rights mentioned in the Constitution and its amendments do not constitute all the possible rights to which the people are entitled. Over the years, the courts have defined "unenumerated" rights, such as the right to vote; the right to move about freely; and, perhaps most controversially, the right to privacy, including the right of a woman to have some control over her health and reproductive decisions.

AMENDMENT X (1791)

The powers not delegated to the United States by the Constitution, nor prohibited by it to the States, are reserved to the States respectively, or to the people.

When the Constitution was presented for ratification to the people of the thirteen independent states, many were surprised—and alarmed—by the extent to which powers previously exercised by the states (for example, taxation and control over commerce) were now to be exercised by the federal government. In the words of Virginia statesman Patrick Henry, the new government was not really "federal" in character but rather a "consolidated government," one which would render the identity and powers of the states meaningless. The Tenth Amendment reserves all powers not specifically given to the federal government by the Constitution (most of which are contained in Article I, Section 8, in the enumeration of the powers of Congress) to the state governments; it was intended to allay fears about the federal government possessing excessive power.

In one sense, the Tenth Amendment is one of the most important features of the Constitution, for it articulates the principle that the federal government is one of specifically delegated powers, and that it should only exercise those powers explicitly enumerated in the Constitution. But in fact, the Tenth Amendment, because of its generality, has not proven to be much of an impediment to the steady expansion of federal power since the time the Constitution was adopted, although opponents of "big government" have in recent years invoked the Tenth Amendment in their arguments with greater frequency.

AMENDMENT XI (1795)

The Judicial power of the United States shall not be construed to extend to any suit in law or equity, commenced or prosecuted against one of the United States by Citizens of another State, or by Citizens or Subjects of any Foreign State.

In 1793 the Supreme Court ruled that it had a right to hear a suit brought by two citizens of South Carolina against the state of

Georgia. Many members of Congress and of the state legislatures vigorously criticized the court's ruling, claiming that the federal courts had no business interfering with the "sovereign immunity" of state courts. The Eleventh Amendment reserved to the individual states the right to hear cases brought against them either by citizens of another state or another country. As is the case with many of the amendments to the Constitution, the Supreme Court has ruled that there are exceptions to this general rule. For example, since 1824 the Supreme Court has held that state government officials are not immune from being sued in a federal court if they act in violation of a right guaranteed by the U.S. Constitution.

AMENDMENT XII (1804)

The Electors shall meet in their respective states and vote by ballot for President and Vice-President, one of whom, at least, shall not be an inhabitant of the same state with themselves; they shall name in their ballots the person voted for as President, and in distinct ballots the person voted for as Vice-President, and they shall make distinct lists of all persons voted for as President, and of all persons voted for as Vice-President and of the number of votes for each, which lists they shall sign and certify, and transmit sealed to the seat of the government of the United States, directed to the President of the Senate.

The President of the Senate shall, in the presence of the Senate and House of Representatives, open all the certificates and the votes shall then be counted.

The person having the greatest Number of votes for President, shall be the President, if such number be a majority of the whole number of Electors appointed; and if no person have such majority, then from the persons having the highest numbers not exceeding three on the list of those voted for as President, the House of Representatives shall choose immediately, by ballot, the President. But in choosing the President, the votes shall be taken by states, the representation from each state having one vote; a quorum for this purpose shall consist of a member or members from two-thirds of the states, and a majority of all the states shall be necessary to a choice. And if the House of Representatives shall not choose a President whenever the right of choice shall devolve upon them, before the fourth day of March next following, then the Vice-President shall act as President, as in the case of the death or other constitutional disability of the President.

The person having the greatest number of votes as Vice-President, shall be the Vice-President, if such number be a majority of the whole number of Electors appointed, and if no person have a majority, then from the two highest numbers on the list, the Senate shall choose the Vice-President; a quorum for the purpose shall consist of two-thirds of the whole number of Senators, and a majority of the whole number shall be necessary to a choice. But no person constitutionally ineligible to the office of President shall be eligible to that of Vice-President of the United States.

When the framers of the Constitution devised the complicated process by which presidential electors would select the nation's president and vice president, they assumed that those electors would run for their offices as individuals, and that the voters would select them on the basis of their individual merits. In that original notion of the way the electoral system would work, it was expected that the electors would each cast two ballots, with no distinction between a presidential and a vice-presidential ballot, and that the person receiving the greatest number of votes would be elected president and the person receiving the next largest number of votes vice president.

The framers of the Constitution did not anticipate the emergence of an organized political party system in which two extraconstitutional political parties, the Federalists and Jeffersonian Republicans, would organize electors (or, in some states, slates of electors) pledged in advance to vote for presidential and vice-presidential candidates as part of a party "ticket." In the election of 1800, the party ticket of Thomas Jefferson (the person whom the Republicans intended as their presidential candidate) and Aaron Burr (the person whom the Republicans intended as their vice-presidential candidate) received a majority of electoral votes. In fact, though, party discipline was so great that the electors cast their votes on their two ballots in such a way that Jefferson and Burr had an equal number of votes, with no constitutional mechanism for deciding which of the candidates was intended to be the presidential candidate and which the vice-presidential candidate. As a consequence, the election was thrown into the House of Representatives, where, after a great deal of intrigue, Jefferson was selected as president and Burr the vice president.

The adoption of the Twelfth Amendment was a necessary adjustment to the way in which the American party system had transformed America's presidential elections. Although the provisions of the Twelfth Amendment are as mind-numbingly complicated as the original provisions of Article II, Section 1, the essential feature of the amendment was that henceforth electors would vote separately for the president and vice president. And while the original language in Article II, Section 1, stipulated that the House of Representatives would choose among the five leading candidates should no one receive a majority of electoral votes, the new provision in the Twelfth Amendment narrowed the choice to the top three candidates.

AMENDMENT XIII (1865)
SECTION 1

Neither slavery nor involuntary servitude, except as a punishment for crime whereof the party shall have been duly convicted, shall exist within the United States, or any place subject to their jurisdiction.

SECTION 2

Congress shall have power to enforce this article by appropriate legislation.

👉 The Thirteenth Amendment was passed by Congress in 1861, as the Southern states were seceding from the union, but not ratified until 1865, after the South had accepted defeat in the Civil War. It marked the first important step in bringing American constitutional practice into harmony with American libertarian values. Although there had been previous, private attempts to eliminate slavery, usually accompanied by promises of compensation for the value of the "property" lost as a consequence of the emancipation of slaves, the Thirteenth Amendment unequivocally abolished slavery, providing for the immediate emancipation of all slaves in the United States, without compensation to their owners. It also gave to Congress the power to enforce the emancipation of slaves, a power that it exercised in the Civil Rights Act of 1866.

AMENDMENT XIV (1868)

SECTION 1

All persons born or naturalized in the United States, and subject to the jurisdiction thereof, are citizens of the United States and of the State wherein they reside. No State shall make or enforce any law which shall abridge the privileges or immunities of citizens of the United States; nor shall any State deprive any person of life, liberty, or property, without due process of law; nor deny to any person within its jurisdiction the equal protection of the laws.

SECTION 2

Representatives shall be apportioned among the several States according to their respective numbers, counting the whole number of persons in each State, excluding Indians not taxed. But when the right to vote at any election for the choice of electors for President and Vice-President of the United States, Representatives in Congress, the Executive and Judicial officers of a State, or the members of the Legislature thereof, is denied to any of the male inhabitants of such State, being twenty-one years of age, and citizens of the United States, or in any way abridged, except for participation in rebellion, or other crime, the basis of representation therein shall be reduced in the proportion which the number of such male citizens shall bear to the whole number of male citizens twenty-one years of age in such State.

SECTION 3

No person shall be a Senator or Representative in Congress, or elector of President and Vice-President, or hold any office, civil or military, under the United States, or under any State, who, having previously taken an oath, as a member of Congress, or as an officer of the United States, or as a member of any State legislature, or as an executive or judicial officer of any State, to support the Constitution of the United States, shall have engaged in insurrection or rebellion against the same, or given aid or comfort to the enemies thereof. But Congress may by a vote of two-thirds of each House, remove such disability.

SECTION 4

The validity of the public debt of the United States, authorized by law, including debts incurred for payment of pensions and bounties for services in suppressing insurrection or rebellion, shall not be questioned. But neither the United States nor any State shall assume or pay any debt or obligation incurred in aid of insurrection or rebellion against the United States, or any claim for the loss or emancipation of any slave; but all such debts, obligations and claims shall be held illegal and void.

Section 5

The Congress shall have power to enforce, by appropriate legislation, the provisions of this article.

Perhaps the most significant and far-reaching amendment to the Constitution, the Fourteenth Amendment is viewed by many scholars and jurists as the provision of the Constitution that has brought the principles enunciated in the preamble of the Declaration of Independence into the realm of constitutional law. The words of the preamble of the Declaration—"that all men are created equal, that they are endowed by their Creator with certain unalienable Rights, that among these are Life, Liberty and the pursuit of Happiness"—are purely exhortatory; they were important rhetorically in defining American purposes as they declared the colonies' independence from Great Britain, but they do not have the force of law. At the heart of the Fourteenth Amendment is the stipulation that all Americans born or naturalized in the United States, including the newly freed slaves, are citizens of the United States, and that no state may make or enforce any law that shall infringe on the rights of American citizens, including those unalienable rights of "life, liberty or property" without due process of law. The Fourteenth Amendment's promise that all persons are guaranteed "equal protection of the laws" would prove an important mechanism by which the Supreme Court, in a series of rulings in the twentieth century, would articulate a uniform standard by which many of the rights spelled out in the Bill of Rights would be guaranteed to all citizens in each of the states.

Section 2 of the Fourteenth Amendment had a more specific intent. It effectively repealed the three-fifths compromise by which slaves were counted as three-fifths of a person in the apportionment of representation and taxation, and stipulates that any state that attempts to deny the right to vote to any male United States citizen over the age of twenty-one will have its representation in Congress and the electoral college reduced proportionally to the number of citizens so disenfranchised. This part of Section 2 was clearly intended by the members of Congress who drafted it as a means of protecting the newly freed slaves' right to vote. It is notable that the only exception to this protection of the right to vote is in the case of individuals who have participated "in rebellion, or other crime." This exception not only applied to convicted criminals (who are still denied the right to vote in most states) but also to large numbers of Americans who had participated in the Southern "rebellion" during the Civil War.

Section 3 of the amendment explicitly excluded former Southern rebels from serving in any federal or state office until Congress, by a two-thirds vote, removed that prohibition. This constitutional device effectively turned over control of the "reconstruction" of the former secessionist states to individuals who had remained loyal to the union during the Civil War.

Section 4 of the amendment absolved the federal government of any responsibility for the debts incurred by the Southern states or by the Confederacy during the Civil War.

Finally, Section 5 granted to Congress broad authority to proceed with legislation that would enforce the provisions of the Fourteenth Amendment. In the immediate aftermath of the adoption of the amendment, Congress passed seven statutes aimed at guaranteeing civil rights to freed slaves as well as imposing conditions for readmission to the union on the states that had seceded from it. Over the course of the next two decades, many of the provisions of those statutes would be ruled unconstitutional by the Supreme Court, which adopted an increasingly narrow interpretation of the rights granted by the Fourteenth Amendment.

AMENDMENT XV (1870)

SECTION 1

The right of citizens of the United States to vote shall not be denied or abridged by the United States or by any State on account of race, color, or previous condition of servitude.

SECTION 2

The Congress shall have the power to enforce this article by appropriate legislation.

☞ While the Fourteenth Amendment punished states that deprived newly freed slaves of the right to vote by reducing their representation in the House of Representatives, the Fifteenth Amendment categorically prohibits the denial of the right to vote on account of race, color, or previous condition of servitude. Notably, the amendment does not mention gender, which, to the dismay of advocates of women's suffrage, meant that although newly freed male slaves were guaranteed a right to vote, women of all races were denied that right. In spite of the adoption of the Fifteenth Amendment, the states of the former Confederacy managed to find ways to continue to drastically curtail the right of African Americans to vote, through the use of poll taxes, literacy tests, and other discriminatory devices. It was not until the passage of the Voting Rights Act of 1965 that African Americans have had equal access to the polling place.

AMENDMENT XVI (1913)

The Congress shall have power to lay and collect taxes on incomes, from whatever source derived, without apportionment among the several States, and without regard to any census or enumeration.

✍ Although the original version of the Constitution gave Congress the power to levy direct taxes, such taxation was only to be levied on the states themselves, in direct proportion to their population. Although Congress during the Civil War was able to levy a direct tax on individuals as part of a wartime measure, the Supreme Court, in an 1895 ruling (*Pollock v. Farmers Loan and Trust Co.*), ruled that taxing the property of individuals was unconstitutional. The Sixteenth Amendment effectively reversed that ruling. It is silent on what the rate of taxation might be (for example, it does not speak to whether all individuals should be taxed at an equal rate or whether the rate of taxation should be progressively higher on higher incomes). Congress, which enacted a federal income tax law in October 1913, just seven months after the passage of the Sixteenth Amendment, opted for a modestly progressive tax rate. The rate of taxation imposed on the top taxation bracket has varied from 7 percent in 1913 to a high of 92 percent in 1952–53. The current rate of taxation in the top bracket is 38.6 percent, nearer the low end of that continuum.

AMENDMENT XVII (1913)

The Senate of the United States shall be composed of two Senators from each State, elected by the people thereof, for six years; and each Senator shall have one vote. The electors in each State shall have the qualifications requisite for electors of the most numerous branch of the State legislatures.

When vacancies happen in the representation of any State in the Senate, the executive authority of such State shall issue writs of election to fill such vacancies: *Provided*, That the legislature of any State may empower the executive thereof to make temporary appointments until the people fill the vacancies by election as the legislature may direct.

This amendment shall not be so construed as to affect the election or term of any Senator chosen before it becomes valid as part of the Constitution.

☞ When the Constitution was first drafted, the framers believed that the Senate, the upper house, should be the repository of superior wisdom and virtue and, toward that end, stipulated that senators should be elected by the legislatures of each of the states, whose members would presumably be able to make a wiser choice than the people at large. As one of a series of reforms during the Progressive Era, Congress proposed, and the states endorsed, an amendment calling for direct, popular election of senators.

AMENDMENT XVIII (1919)
Section 1

After one year from the ratification of this article the manufacture, sale, or transportation of intoxicating liquors within, the importation thereof into, or the exportation thereof from the United States and all territory subject to the jurisdiction thereof for beverage purposes is hereby prohibited.

Section 2

The Congress and the several States shall have concurrent power to enforce this article by appropriate legislation.

Section 3

This article shall be inoperative unless it shall have been ratified as an amendment to the Constitution by the legislatures of the several States, as provided in the Constitution, within seven years from the date of the submission hereof to the States by the Congress.

☞ Most of the amendments to the Constitution seek to grant specific rights to the people by placing restraints on the actions of the government. The Eighteenth Amendment is the only amendment that has sought to restrict the rights of the people—in this case the right to manufacture, sell, or transport "intoxicating liquors" within the United States. Interestingly, it does not prevent the consumption of liquor. Though liquor consumption declined markedly during the years when the amendment was in force, it certainly did not cease. Indeed, as people turned to illegal sources for their alcoholic beverages, the operation of the Eighteenth Amendment served to encourage otherwise law-abiding people to break the law and bolster the activities of organized crime.

AMENDMENT XIX (1920)

The right of citizens of the United States to vote shall not be denied or abridged by the United States or by any State on account of sex.

Congress shall have power to enforce this article by appropriate legislation.

☞ The Nineteenth Amendment was the culmination of more than three-quarters of a century of dedicated work by advocates of female suffrage. Although some states had passed legislation allowing women the right to vote prior to 1920, that right was not extended to all women until the adoption of the Nineteenth Amendment. Unlike the operation of the Fifteenth Amendment, which was thwarted by states that found ways to continue to deny the vote to African Americans, the amendment granting women the right to vote encountered little resistance in the aftermath of its passage.

AMENDMENT XX (1933)

SECTION 1

The terms of the President and Vice President shall end at noon on the 20th day of January, and the terms of Senators and Representatives at noon on the 3d day of January, of the years in which such terms would have ended if this article had not been ratified; and the terms of their successors shall then begin.

SECTION 2

The Congress shall assemble at least once in every year, and such meeting shall begin at noon on the 3d day of January, unless they shall by law appoint a different day.

SECTION 3

If, at the time fixed for the beginning of the term of the President, the President elect shall have died, the Vice President elect shall become President. If a President shall not have been chosen before the time fixed for the beginning of his term, or if the President elect shall have failed to qualify, then the Vice President elect shall act as President until a President shall have qualified; and the Congress may by law provide for the case wherein neither a President elect nor a Vice President elect shall have qualified, declaring who shall then act as President, or the manner in which one who is to act shall be selected, and such person shall act accordingly until a President or Vice President shall have qualified.

SECTION 4

The Congress may by law provide for the case of the death of any of the persons from whom the House of Representatives may choose a President whenever the right of choice shall have devolved upon them, and for the case of the death of any of the persons from whom the Senate may choose a Vice President whenever the right of choice shall have devolved upon them.

SECTION 5

Sections 1 and 2 shall take effect on the 15th day of October following the ratification of this article.

SECTION 6

This article shall be inoperative unless it shall have been ratified as an amendment to the Constitution by the legislatures of three-fourths of the several States within seven years from the date of its submission.

🖙 Many of the most consequential amendments to the Constitution (e.g., the first ten amendments) are remarkably brief, while some of the more arcane amendments seem to require more elaborate verbiage. This is certainly the case with the Twentieth Amendment.

Traditionally, new presidents took office in March, creating a significant time gap between their election in November and their inauguration. In some cases, this time lag had serious consequences. For example, during the period between Abraham Lincoln's election and inauguration, his Democratic predecessor, James Buchanan, found himself to be a lame-duck president at a time when Southern states were seceding from the union. In recognition of the improvements in communication and transportation since the Constitution was originally adopted, the Twentieth Amendment reduced the amount of time elapsing between the president's election and his inauguration. It also moved the meeting time of a newly elected Congress from March to January 3, preventing the meeting of a lame-duck session of Congress whose actions might not be consonant with the will of the electorate as expressed in the November elections.

The remaining parts of the Twentieth Amendment seek to clarify the role of Congress in determining a plan of succession in case of the death or removal of both the president and vice president. For much of the nineteenth century, Congress designated the president pro tempore of the Senate as next in line of succession; from the 1880s until 1947, Congress stipulated that the secretary of state would be next in line. The decision to change the law and provide for the Speaker of the House to assume office in case of the president and vice president's absence was shaped by the desire to have a popularly elected official—in this case the leader of the legislative branch most directly responsible to the people— assume the presidency.

AMENDMENT XXI (1933)
SECTION 1

The eighteenth article of amendment to the Constitution of the United States is hereby repealed.

SECTION 2

The transportation or importation into any State, Territory, or Possession of the United States for delivery or use therein of intoxicating liquors, in violation of the laws thereof, is hereby prohibited.

SECTION 3

The article shall be inoperative unless it shall have been ratified as an amendment to the Constitution by conventions in the several States, as provided in the Constitution, within seven years from the date of the submission hereof to the States by the Congress.

> Just as the Eighteenth Amendment is the only constitutional amendment to restrict the rights of the American people, the Twenty-first Amendment, which ended Prohibition, is the only amendment in the Constitution to repeal a previous amendment. The Twenty-first Amendment does not specifically allow for the manufacture, transport, or sale of liquors but, rather, returns to the states the right to regulate alcohol distribution and consumption. This amendment is unusual in that it specifies that state conventions, rather than state legislatures, should be the bodies responsible for ratifying the amendment.

AMENDMENT XXII (1951)

SECTION 1

No person shall be elected to the office of the President more than twice, and no person who has held the office of President, or acted as President, for more than two years of a term to which some other person was elected President shall be elected to the office of President more than once. But this Article shall not apply to any person holding the office of President when this Article was proposed by the Congress, and shall not prevent any person who may be holding the office of President, or acting as President, during the term within which this Article becomes operative from holding the office of President or acting as President during the remainder of such term.

SECTION 2

This article shall be inoperative unless it shall have been ratified as an amendment to the Constitution by the legislatures of three-fourths of the several States within seven years from the date of its submission to the States by the Congress.

✍ Although the people of the United States had expressed their will by electing Franklin D. Roosevelt president in four successive elections, in the aftermath of Roosevelt's terms in office many Americans began to have second thoughts about the wisdom of allowing a president to exceed what had previously been the "two-term tradition" set by George Washington. By the terms of the Twenty-second Amendment, Presidents are limited to two terms, or if they have served at least two years of a previous president's term, to one term. Americans continue to disagree on whether "term limits"—either in the executive or legislative branches—are consistent with democratic governance, and there have been occasional attempts to repeal the Twenty-second Amendment, although none has come close to success thus far.

AMENDMENT XXIII (1961)
SECTION 1

The District constituting the seat of Government of the United States shall appoint in such manner as the Congress may direct:

A number of electors of President and Vice President equal to the whole number of Senators and Representatives in Congress to which the District would be entitled if it were a State, but in no event more than the least populous State; they shall be in addition to those appointed by the States, but they shall be considered, for the purposes of the election of President and Vice President, to be electors appointed by a State; and they shall meet in the District and perform such duties as provided by the twelfth article of amendment.

SECTION 2

The Congress shall have power to enforce this article by appropriate legislation.

☞ The District of Columbia, seat of the nation's government, has always occupied a peculiar place within our federal system. The Constitution empowered Congress to designate a territory "not exceeding ten Miles square" as the nation's capital but specifically intended that the "federal district" not be within the boundaries or jurisdiction of any particular state. Therefore, while the federal government exercises much of its enormous power within the District of Columbia, that territory has been denied voting representatives in Congress, and until the passage of the Twenty-third Amendment, its residents were denied the right to vote in presidential elections. By the terms of the Twenty-third Amendment the residents of the District of Columbia are entitled to vote for presidential electors, with the number of electors representing the district being equal to the number of senators and representatives that the district would have if it were a state. On the basis of its present population, that means three electors.

AMENDMENT XXIV (1964)
SECTION 1

The right of citizens of the United States to vote in any primary or other election for President or Vice President, for electors for President or Vice President, or for Senator or Representative in Congress, shall not be denied or abridged by the United States or any State by reason of failure to pay any poll tax or other tax.

SECTION 2

The Congress shall have power to enforce this article by appropriate legislation.

☞ Although the Fourteenth and Fifteenth Amendments were intended to ensure African Americans the right to vote, the imposition of a poll tax—a fee that citizens had to pay to the state or locality if they wished to vote—was a common device by which states, particularly those in the South, prevented low-income voters, who were often predominantly African American, from voting. The Twenty-fourth Amendment explicitly prohibits the imposition of taxes as a condition for voting. The amendment does not say anything about the use of the poll tax in state elections, but soon after the passage of the Twenty-fourth Amendment, the Supreme Court, citing the "equal protection" clause of the Fourteenth Amendment, ruled that it was unconstitutional for states to require the payment of poll taxes as a condition for voting in state elections.

AMENDMENT XXV (1967)

SECTION 1

In case of the removal of the President from office or of his death or resignation, the Vice President shall become President.

SECTION 2

Whenever there is a vacancy in the office of the Vice President, the President shall nominate a Vice President who shall take office upon confirmation by a majority vote of both Houses of Congress.

SECTION 3

Whenever the President transmits to the President pro tempore of the Senate and the Speaker of the House of Representatives his written declaration that he is unable to discharge the powers and duties of his office, and until he transmits to them a written declaration to the contrary, such powers and duties shall be discharged by the Vice President as Acting President.

SECTION 4

Whenever the Vice President and a majority of either the principal officers of the executive departments or of such other body as Congress may by law provide, transmit to the President pro tempore of the Senate and the Speaker of the House of Representatives their written declaration that the President is unable to discharge the powers and duties of his office, the Vice President shall immediately assume the powers and duties of the office as Acting President.

Thereafter, when the President transmits to the President pro tempore of the Senate and the Speaker of the House of Representatives his written declaration that no inability exists, he shall resume the powers and duties of his office unless the Vice President and a majority of either the principal officers of the executive department or of such other body as Congress may by law provide, transmit within four days to the President pro tempore of the Senate and the Speaker of the House of Representatives their written declaration that the President is unable to discharge the powers and duties of his office. Thereupon Congress shall decide the issue, assembling within forty-eight hours for that purpose if not in session. If the Congress, within twenty-one days after receipt of the latter written declaration, or, if Congress is not in session, within twenty-one days after Congress is required to assemble, determines by two-thirds vote of both Houses that the President is unable to discharge the powers and duties of his office, the Vice President shall continue to discharge the same as Acting President; otherwise, the President shall resume the powers and duties of his office.

✒ Although the Twentieth Amendment deals in part with the issue of presidential succession, the Twenty-fifth Amendment provides a more detailed description of how Congress should proceed in the event of the death or removal of a president or vice president, or in the case of the temporary disability of the president (for example, if the president falls seriously ill or undergoes an operation and is not able for a period of time to exercise the duties of his office). Eight American presidents have died in office, and one has resigned. And there have been several occasions when a president has been temporarily disabled (for example, when Ronald Reagan was wounded by a would-be assassin's bullet in 1985, he transferred power to his vice president, George H. W. Bush, while he was hospitalized).

The amendment also deals with the delicate question of how to deal with the disability of a president when the president himself is not willing to declare such a disability. For example, in 1918 President Woodrow Wilson suffered a stroke and many believed that his disability prevented him from carrying out the duties of his office effectively, but there were no means by which to resolve the issue. The Twenty-sixth Amendment stipulates that Congress may, if two-thirds of the members of both houses agree, provide written declaration that the president is disabled and then transfer power to the vice president.

AMENDMENT XXVI (1971)

SECTION 1

The right of citizens of the United States, who are eighteen years of age or older, to vote shall not be denied or abridged by the United States or by any State on account of age.

SECTION 2

The Congress shall have power to enforce this article by appropriate legislation.

> ✥ It is no accident that this amendment giving citizens eighteen years or older the right to vote was passed at the height of the Vietnam War. Some of the reasoning behind the amendment was that if young men and women are old enough to serve and risk their lives in the military, then they should also be given the right to vote.

AMENDMENT XXVII (1992)

No law, varying the compensation for the services of the Senators and Representatives, shall take effect, until an election of Representatives shall have intervened.

> ✥ The Twenty-seventh Amendment was originally part of the package of twelve amendments submitted to the states by the First Congress in 1789, but it was not ratified at that time. Agitation to reconsider the amendment resurfaced in the 1980s, as the public became increasingly unhappy over a series of pay raises that members of Congress awarded themselves. The provisions of this amendment make it impossible for members of Congress to put into effect increases in their salaries before the session in which they are serving has ended. By this mechanism, members of Congress seeking reelection have to justify their proposed increases in salary to voters during their reelection campaigns.

SELECTIONS FROM
THE FEDERALIST
PAPERS

THE EIGHTY-FIVE ESSAYS appearing in New York City newspapers under the pseudonym Publius between October 1787 and May 1788 and later published as a single collection under the title *The Federalist Papers* have achieved justifiable fame as an important statement of American constitutional philosophy. Alexander Hamilton took the lead, recruiting James Madison and John Jay to join him in the effort. In all, Hamilton wrote fifty-one of the essays, Madison twenty-nine, and Jay five. The essays were written independently, with little collaboration among the three authors. Indeed, they were written under such constraints that there was seldom time for review or revision.

Looking at *The Federalist Papers* as a whole, one can see that Madison tended to write his essays on general issues of government and politics—on republicanism and representation in particular—while Hamilton focused on specific issues, such as taxation or the construction of the executive and judiciary. It is perhaps for that reason that Madison's essays, though constituting only about a third of the total, are the ones most often quoted and reprinted.

The Federalist Papers have grown more influential over time and have come to be considered an important means of understanding the intent of the framers of the Constitution. In the period between 1790 and 1800, when leaders of the new republic were facing the challenge of creating a government that conformed to the precepts of their new Constitution, *The Federalist* (the original published collection containing seventy-seven of the essays) was cited by the Supreme Court only once. In the whole of the nineteenth century, the essays were cited 58 times. In the first half of the twentieth century, they were cited 38 times, but in the last half they were cited no fewer than 194 times.

However much *The Federalist Papers* may on some occasions rise to the level of high-minded political theory, readers should also be aware that they were initially intended as political propaganda. Madison and Hamilton, whatever their intellectual gifts, were also practical politicians with a specific goal: to secure ratification of the Constitution. In that sense, *The Federalist Papers*, like the Constitution they were defending, need to be understood not merely as abstract constitutional treatises but also as a product of the give-and-take of the turbulent era of eighteenth-century American politics.

This volume reprints the three *Federalist* essays that many scholars consider to be the most important of the eighty-five. "Federalist No. 10," which deals with the benefits of an "extended republic" in controlling the effects of "faction," and "Federalist No. 51," which lays out the doctrine of "separation of powers," were written by Madison. "Federalist No. 78," written by Hamilton, is not only a defense of an independent judiciary but also lays out the constitutional argument for what would later be called "judicial review." The essays are presented in slightly abridged form.

FEDERALIST NO. 10:
JAMES MADISON,
NOVEMBER 22, 1787

☞ One of the most famous pieces of writing in all American history, "Federalist No. 10" takes a distinctly modern approach to the existence of "faction" and "interests" in American politics. Whereas most eighteenth-century commentators believed that the key to good government was to elect virtuous political leaders capable of transcending their own selfish interests, Madison accepted the existence of conflicting interests as an inherent part of any pluralist society. The best way to control the effects of faction, Madison argued, was to extend the sphere of government over a sufficiently large territory so that no one faction could obtain undue influence and subvert the public good.

Among the numerous advantages promised by a well constructed Union, none deserves to be more accurately developed than its tendency to break and control the violence of faction. The friend of popular governments never finds himself so much alarmed for their character and fate, as when he contemplates their propensity to this dangerous vice. He will not fail, therefore, to set a due value on any plan which, without violating the principles to which he is attached, provides a proper cure for it. The instability, injustice, and confusion introduced into the public councils, have in truth been the mortal diseases under which popular governments have everywhere perished; as they continue to be the favorite and fruitful topics from which the adversaries to liberty derive their most specious declamations. The valuable improvements made by the American Constitutions on the popular models, both ancient and modern, cannot certainly be too much admired; but it would be an unwarrantable partiality, to contend that they have as effectually obviated the danger on this side as was wished and expected. Complaints are every where heard from our most considerate and virtuous citizens, equally the friends of public and private faith, and of public and personal liberty, that our governments are too unstable; that the public good is disregarded in the conflicts of rival parties; and that measures are too often decided, not according to the rules of justice and the rights of the minor party; but by the superior force of an interested and overbearing majority. However anxiously we may wish that these complaints had no foundation, the evidence of known facts will not permit us to deny that they are in some degree true. . . .

By a faction, I understand a number of citizens, whether amounting to a majority or a minority of the whole, who are united and actuated by some common impulse of passion, or of interest, adverse to the rights of other citizens, or to the permanent and aggregate interests of the community.

There are two methods of curing the mischiefs of faction: the one, by removing its causes; the other, by controlling its effects.

There are again two methods of removing the causes of faction: the one, by destroying the liberty which is essential to its existence; the other, by giving to every citizen the same opinions, the same passions, and the same interests.

It could never be more truly said than of the first remedy, that it is worse than the disease. Liberty is to faction, what air is to fire, an aliment without which it instantly expires. But it could not be a less folly to abolish liberty, which is essential to political life, because it nourishes faction, than it would be to wish the annihilation of air, which is essential to animal life, because it imparts to fire its destructive agency.

The second expedient is as impracticable, as the first would be unwise. As long as the reason of man continues fallible, and he is at liberty to exercise it, different opinions will be formed. As long as the connection subsists between his reason and his self-love, his opinions and his passions will have a reciprocal influence on each other; and the former will be objects to which the latter will attach themselves. The diversity in the faculties of men from which the rights of property originate, is not less an insuperable obstacle to a uniformity of interests. The protection of these faculties is the first object of Government. From the protection of different and unequal faculties of acquiring property, the possession of different degrees and kinds of property immediately results: and from the influence of these on the sentiments and views of the respective proprietors, ensues a division of the society into different interests and parties.

The latent causes of faction are thus sown in the nature of man; and we see them everywhere brought into different degrees of activity, according to the different circumstances of civil society. A zeal for different opinions concerning religion, concerning Government, and many other points, as well of speculation as of practice; an attachment to different leaders ambitiously contending for preeminence and power; or to persons of other descriptions whose fortunes have been interesting to the human passions, have in turn divided mankind into parties, inflamed them with mutual animosity, and rendered them much more disposed to vex and oppress each other than to cooperate for their common good. So strong is this propensity of mankind to fall into mutual animosities, that where no substantial occasion presents itself, the most frivolous and fanciful distinctions have been sufficient to kindle their unfriendly passions, and excite their most violent conflicts. But the most common and durable source of factions, has been the various and unequal distribution of property. Those who hold, and those who are without property, have ever formed distinct interests in society. Those who are creditors, and those who are debtors, fall under a like discrimination. A landed interest, a manufacturing interest, a mercantile interest, a moneyed interest, with many lesser interests, grow up of necessity in civilized nations, and divide them into different classes, actuated by different sentiments and views. The regulation of these various and interfering interests forms the principal task of modern Legislation, and involves the spirit of party and faction in the necessary and ordinary operations of Government. . . .

It is in vain to say, that enlightened statesmen will be able to adjust these clashing interests, and render them all subservient to the public good. Enlightened statesmen will not always be at the helm. Nor, in many cases, can such an adjustment be made at all without taking into view indirect and remote considerations, which will rarely prevail over the immediate interest which one party may find in disregarding the rights of another or the good of the whole.

The inference to which we are brought is, that the *causes* of faction cannot be removed; and that relief is only to be sought in the means of controlling its *effects*.

If a faction consists of less than a majority, relief is supplied by the republican principle, which enables the majority to defeat its sinister views by regular vote: It may clog the administration, it may convulse the society; but it will be unable to execute and mask its violence under the forms of the Constitution. When a majority is included in a faction, the form of popular government on the other hand enables it to sacrifice to its ruling passion or interest, both the public good and the rights of other citizens. To secure the public good, and private rights, against the danger of such a faction, and at the same time to preserve the spirit and the form of popular government, is then the great object to which our inquiries are directed. . . .

By what means is this object attainable? Evidently by

one of two only. Either the existence of the same passion or interest in a majority at the same time, must be prevented; or the majority, having such co-existent passion or interest, must be rendered, by their number and local situation, unable to concert and carry into effect schemes of oppression. . . .

From this view of the subject, it may be concluded that a pure Democracy, by which I mean, a Society, consisting of a small number of citizens, who assemble and administer the Government in person, can admit of no cure for the mischiefs of faction. A common passion or interest will, in almost every case, be felt by a majority of the whole; a communication and concert result from the form of Government itself; and there is nothing to check the inducements to sacrifice the weaker party, or an obnoxious individual. Hence it is, that such Democracies have ever been spectacles of turbulence and contention; have ever been found incompatible with personal security, or the rights of property; and have in general been as short in their lives, as they have been violent in their deaths. Theoretic politicians, who have patronized this species of Government, have erroneously supposed, that by reducing mankind to a perfect equality in their political rights, they would, at the same time, be perfectly equalized and assimilated in their possessions, their opinions, and their passions.

A Republic, by which I mean a Government in which the scheme of representation takes place, opens a different prospect, and promises the cure for which we are seeking. Let us examine the points in which it varies from pure Democracy, and we shall comprehend both the nature of the cure, and the efficacy which it must derive from the Union.

The two great points of difference between a Democracy and a Republic are, first, the delegation of the Government, in the latter, to a small number of citizens elected by the rest; secondly, the greater number of citizens, and greater sphere of country, over which the latter may be extended.

The effect of the first difference is, on the one hand to refine and enlarge the public views, by passing them through the medium of a chosen body of citizens, whose wisdom may best discern the true interest of their country, and whose patriotism and love of justice will be least likely to sacrifice it to temporary or partial considerations. Under such a regulation, it may well happen that the public voice pronounced by the representatives of the people, will be more consonant to the public good, than if pronounced by the people themselves convened for the purpose. On the other hand, the effect may be inverted. Men of factious tempers, of local prejudices, or of sinister designs, may by intrigue, by corruption, or by other means, first obtain the suffrages, and then betray the interests of the people. The question resulting is, whether small or extensive Republics are more favorable to the election of proper guardians of the public weal: and it is clearly decided in favor of the latter by two obvious considerations.

In the first place, it is to be remarked that however small the Republic may be, the Representatives must be raised to a certain number, in order to guard against the cabals of a few; and that however large it may be, they must be limited to a certain number, in order to guard against the confusion of a multitude. Hence the number of Representatives in the two cases, not being in proportion to that of the Constituents, and being proportionally greater in the small Republic, it follows, that if the proportion of fit characters, be not less, in the large than in the small Republic, the former will present a greater option, and consequently a greater probability of a fit choice.

In the next place, as each Representative will be chosen

by a greater number of citizens in the large than in the small Republic, it will be more difficult for unworthy candidates to practice with success the vicious arts, by which elections are too often carried; and the suffrages of the people being more free, will be more likely to centre on men who possess the most attractive merit and the most diffusive and established characters.

It must be confessed, that in this, as in most other cases, there is a mean, on both sides of which inconveniences will be found to lie. By enlarging too much the number of electors, you render the representatives too little acquainted with all their local circumstances and lesser interests; as by reducing it too much, you render him unduly attached to these, and too little fit to comprehend and pursue great and national objects. The Federal Constitution forms a happy combination in this respect; the great and aggregate interests being referred to the national, the local and particular, to the state legislatures.

The other point of difference is, the greater number of citizens and extent of territory which may be brought within the compass of Republican, than of Democratic Government; and it is this circumstance principally which renders factious combinations less to be dreaded in the former, than in the latter. The smaller the society, the fewer probably will be the distinct parties and interests composing it; the fewer the distinct parties and interests, the more frequently will a majority be found of the same party; and the smaller the number of individuals composing a majority, and the smaller the compass within which they are placed, the more easily will they concert and execute their plans of oppression. Extend the sphere, and you take in a greater variety of parties and interests; you make it less probable that a majority of the whole will have a common motive to invade the rights of other citizens; or if such a common motive exists, it will be more difficult for all who feel it to discover their own strength, and to act in unison with each other. . . .

Hence it clearly appears, that the same advantage, which a Republic has over a Democracy, in controlling the effects of faction, is enjoyed by a large over a small Republic—is enjoyed by the Union over the States composing it. Does the advantage consist in the substitution of Representatives whose enlightened views and virtuous sentiments render them superior to local prejudices and schemes of injustice? It will not be denied, that the Representation of the Union will be most likely to possess these requisite endowments. Does it consist in the greater security afforded by a greater variety of parties, against the event of any one party being able to outnumber and oppress the rest? In an equal degree does the encreased variety of parties comprised within the Union, encrease this security. Does it, in fine, consist in the greater obstacles opposed to the concert and accomplishment of the secret wishes of an unjust and interested majority? Here, again, the extent of the Union gives it the most palpable advantage.

The influence of factious leaders may kindle a flame within their particular States, but will be unable to spread a general conflagration through the other States; a religious sect, may degenerate into a political faction in a part of the Confederacy; but the variety of sects dispersed over the entire face of it, must secure the national Councils against any danger from that source: a rage for paper money, for an abolition of debts, for an equal division of property, or for any other improper or wicked project, will be less apt to pervade the whole body of the Union, than a particular member of it; in the same proportion as such a malady is more likely to taint a particular county or district, than an entire State.

In the extent and proper structure of the Union, therefore, we behold a Republican remedy for the diseases most incident to Republican Government. And according to the degree of pleasure and pride we feel in being Republicans, ought to be our zeal in cherishing the spirit and supporting the character of Federalists.

PUBLIUS

FEDERALIST NO. 51: JAMES MADISON, FEBRUARY 6, 1788

Madison hoped that the new federal government would be strong and energetic, but at the same time he wished to prevent any one branch of the government from becoming *too* powerful. "If angels were to govern men," Madison reasoned, then "neither external nor internal controuls on government would be necessary." But since the tendency of all men, and of all branches of government, is to attempt to increase their power, it was necessary to devise structures within the federal government to prevent excessive concentrations of power. "Ambition must be made to counteract ambition," Madison asserted, and the way to do this was to create a system of government in which each branch of that government operated in its appropriate sphere, serving at the same time as a check on the other branches.

To what expedient then shall we finally resort for maintaining in practice the necessary partition of power among the several departments, as laid down in the Constitution? The only answer that can be given is, that as all these exterior provisions are found to be inadequate, the defect must be supplied, by so contriving the interior structure of the government, as that its several constituent parts may, by their mutual relations, be the means of keeping each other in their proper places. Without presuming to undertake a full development of this important idea, I will hazard a few general observations, which may perhaps place it in a clearer light, and enable us to form a more correct judgment of the principles and structure of the government planned by the convention.

In order to lay a due foundation for that separate and distinct exercise of the different powers of government, which to a certain extent, is admitted on all hands to be essential to the preservation of liberty, it is evident that each department should have a will of its own; and consequently should be so constituted that the members of each should have as little agency as possible in the appointment of the members of the others. Were this principle rigorously adhered to, it would require that all the appointments for the supreme executive, legislative, and judiciary magistracies, should be drawn from the same fountain of authority, the people, through channels having no communication whatever with one another. Perhaps such a plan of constructing the several departments would be less difficult in practice than it may in contemplation appear. Some difficulties, however, and some additional expence, would attend the execution of it. Some deviations therefore from the principle must be admitted. In the constitution of the judiciary department in particular, it might be inexpedient to insist rigorously on the principle; first, because peculiar qualifications being essential in the members, the primary consideration ought to be to select that mode of choice, which best secures these qualifications; secondly, because the permanent tenure by which the appointments are held in that department, must soon destroy all sense of dependence on the authority conferring them.

It is equally evident that the members of each department should be as little dependent as possible on those of the others, for the emoluments annexed to their offices. Were the executive magistrate, or the judges, not independent of the legislature in this particular, their independence in every other would be merely nominal.

But the great security against a gradual concentration of the several powers in the same department, consists in giving to those who administer each department, the necessary constitutional means and personal motives, to resist encroachments of the others. The provision for defence must in this, as in all other cases, be made commensurate to the danger of attack. Ambition must be made to counteract ambition. The interest of the man must be connected with the constitutional rights of the place. It may be a reflection on human nature, that such devices should be necessary to control the abuses of government. But what is government itself but the greatest of all reflections on human nature? If men were angels, no government would be necessary. If angels were to govern men, neither external nor internal controuls on government would be necessary. In framing a government which is to be administered by men over men, the great difficulty lies in this: You must first enable the government to controul the governed; and in the next place oblige it to controul itself. A dependence on the people is no doubt the primary controul on the government; but experience has taught mankind the necessity of auxiliary precautions.

This policy of supplying by opposite and rival interests, the defect of better motives, might be traced through the whole system of human affairs, private as well as public. We see it particularly displayed in all the subordinate distributions of power; where the constant aim is to divide and arrange the several offices in such a manner as that each may be a check on the other; that the private interest of every individual may be a sentinel over the public rights. These inventions of prudence cannot be less requisite in the distribution of the supreme powers of the state.

But it is not possible to give to each department an equal

power of self-defence. In republican government, the legislative authority, necessarily, predominates. The remedy for this inconveniency is, to divide the legislature into different branches; and to render them, by different modes of election and different principles of action, as little connected with each other, as the nature of their common functions, and their common dependence on the society, will admit. It may even be necessary to guard against dangerous encroachments by still further precautions. As the weight of the legislative authority requires that it should be thus divided, the weakness of the executive may require, on the other hand, that it should be fortified. An absolute negative on the legislature appears at first view to be the natural defence with which the executive magistrate should be armed. But perhaps it would be neither altogether safe, nor alone sufficient. On ordinary occasions, it might not be exerted with the requisite firmness; and on extraordinary occasions, it might be perfidiously abused. May not this defect of an absolute negative be supplied, by some qualified connection between this weaker department, and the weaker branch of the stronger department, by which the latter may be led to support the constitutional rights of the former, without being too much detached from the rights of its own department? . . .

There are moreover two considerations particularly applicable to the federal system of America, which place that system in a very interesting point of view.

First. In a single republic, all the power surrendered by the people, is submitted to the administration of a single government; and the usurpations are guarded against by a division of the government into distinct and separate departments. In the compound republic of America, the power surrendered by the people, is first divided between two distinct governments, and then the portion allotted to each, subdivided among distinct and separate departments. Hence a double security arises to the rights of the people. The different governments will controul each other; at the same time that each will be controuled by itself.

Second. It is of great importance in a republic, not only to guard the society against the oppression of its rulers; but to guard one part of the society against the injustice of the other part. Different interests necessarily exist in different classes of citizens. If a majority be united by a common interest, the rights of the minority will be insecure. There are but two methods of providing against this evil: The one by creating a will in the community independent of the majority, that is, of the society itself; the other by comprehending in the society so many separate descriptions of citizens, as will render an unjust combination of a majority of the whole, very improbable, if not impracticable. The first method prevails in all governments possessing an hereditary or self-appointed authority. This at best is but a precarious security; because a power independent of the society may as well espouse the unjust views of the major, as the rightful interests, of the minor party, and may possibly be turned against both parties. The second method will be exemplified in the federal republic of the United States. Whilst all authority in it will be derived from and dependent on the society, the society itself will be broken into so many parts, interests, and classes of citizens, that the rights of individuals or of the minority, will be in little danger from interested combinations of the majority. In a free government, the security for civil rights must be the same as that for religious rights. It consists in the one case in the multiplicity of interests, and in the other in the multiplicity of sects. The degree of security in both cases will depend on the number of interests and sects; and this may be presumed to depend on the extent of country and number of people comprehended under the same government. This view of the subject must particularly recommend a proper federal system to all the sincere and considerate friends of republican government: Since it shews that in exact proportion as the territory of the Union may be formed into more circumscribed confederacies or states, oppressive combinations of a majority will be facilitated, the best security under the republican forms, for the rights of every class of citizens, will be diminished; and consequently, the stability and independence of some member of the government, the only other security, must be proportionately increased. Justice is the end of government. It is the end of civil society. It ever has been, and ever will be pursued, until it be obtained, or until liberty be lost in the pursuit. In a society under the forms of which the stronger faction can readily unite and oppress the weaker, anarchy may as truly be said to reign, as in a state of nature where the weaker individual is not secured against the violence of the stronger: And as in the latter state even the stronger individuals are prompted by the uncertainty of their condition, to submit to a government which may protect the weak as well as themselves: So in the former state, will the more powerful factions or parties be gradually induced by a like motive, to wish for a government which will protect all parties, the weaker as well as the more powerful. . . . In the extended republic of the United States, and among the great variety of interests, parties, and sects which it embraces, a coalition of a majority of the whole society could seldom take place on any other principles than those of justice and the general good; and there being thus less danger to a minor from the will of a major party, there must be less pretext also, to provide for the security of the former, by introducing into the government a will not dependent on the latter; or in other words, a will independent of the society itself. It is no less certain than it is important, notwithstanding the contrary opinions which have been entertained, that the larger the society, provided it lie within a practical sphere, the more duly capable it will be of self-government. And happily for the *republican cause*, the practicable sphere may be carried to a very great extent, by a judicious modification and mixture of the *federal principle*.

PUBLIUS

FEDERALIST NO. 78:
ALEXANDER HAMILTON,
MAY 28, 1788

🖙 "Federalist No. 78" is Alexander Hamilton's most significant contribution to *The Federalist Papers*. The principle topic of the essay is the importance of protecting the "weakest of the three departments" of government, the judiciary, from encroachments by the executive and, in particular, the legislative branches. Hamilton's solution to this problem was to create a judicial branch that could operate as independently of influence from the other two branches of government as possible. The best way to do this, he argues, is to appoint federal judges for a term of "good behaviour"—in effect, for life.

In the course of his argument supporting lifetime terms for federal judges, Hamilton states explicitly what many of the Founding Fathers had long believed but had not written into the Constitution: "The interpretation of the laws is the proper and peculiar province of the courts. A constitution is in fact, and must be, regarded by the judges as the fundamental law. It therefore belongs to them to ascertain its meaning as well as the meaning of any particular act proceeding from the legislative body." This assertion of the right of "judicial review" would not be established as a constitutional precedent until the Supreme Court rendered its decision in *Marbury v. Madison* in 1803, but it was an important portent of constitutional developments to come.

We proceed now to an examination of the judiciary department of the proposed government.

In unfolding the defects of the existing confederation, the utility and necessity of a federal judicature have been clearly pointed out. It is the less necessary to recapitulate the considerations there urged; as the propriety of the institution in the abstract is not disputed: The only questions which have been raised being relative to the manner of constituting it, and to its extent. To these points therefore our observations shall be confined.

The manner of constituting it seems to embrace these several objects — 1st. The mode of appointing the judges. 2d. The tenure by which they are to hold their places. 3d. The partition of the judiciary authority between different courts, and their relations to each other. . . .

According to the plan of the convention, all judges who may be appointed by the United States are to hold their offices *during good behaviour*, which is conformable to the most approved of the state constitutions; and among the rest, to that of this state. . . . The standard of good behaviour for the continuance in office of the judicial magistracy is certainly one of the most valuable of the modern improvements in the practice of government. In a monarchy it is an excellent barrier to the despotism of the prince: In a republic it is a no less excellent barrier to the encroachments and oppressions of the representative body. And it is the best expedient which can be devised in any government, to secure a steady, upright, and impartial administration of the laws.

Whoever attentively considers the different departments of power must perceive, that in a government in which they are separated from each other, the judiciary, from the nature of its functions, will always be the least dangerous to the political rights of the Constitution; because it will be least in a capacity to annoy or injure them. The executive not only dispenses the honors, but holds the sword of the community. The legislature not only commands the purse, but prescribes the rules by which the duties and rights of every citizen are to be regulated. The judiciary on the contrary has no influence over either the sword or the purse, no direction either of the strength or of the wealth of the society, and can take no active resolution whatever. It may truly be said to have neither Force nor Will, but merely judgment; and must ultimately depend upon the aid of the executive arm even for the efficacy of its judgments.

This simple view of the matter suggests several important consequences. It proves incontestably that the judiciary is beyond comparison the weakest of the three departments of power; that it can never attack with success either of the other two; and that all possible care is requisite to enable it to defend itself against their attacks. It equally proves, that though individual oppression may now and then proceed from the courts of justice, the general liberty of the people can never be endangered from that quarter: . . . And it proves, in the last place, that . . . from the natural feebleness of the judiciary, it is in continual jeopardy of being overpowered, awed, or influenced by its co-ordinate branches; and that as nothing can contribute so much to its firmness and independence, as permanency in office, this quality may therefore be justly regarded as an indispensable ingredient in its constitution; and in a great measure as the citadel of the public justice and the public security. . . .

Some perplexity respecting the rights of the courts to pronounce legislative acts void, because contrary to the Constitution, has arisen from an imagination that the doctrine would imply a superiority of the judiciary to the legislative power. It is urged that the authority which can declare the acts of another void, must necessarily be superior to the one whose acts may be declared void. As this doctrine is of great importance in all the American constitutions, a brief discussion of the ground on which it rests cannot be unacceptable.

There is no position which depends on clearer principles, than that every act of a delegated authority, contrary to the tenor of the commission under which it is exercised, is void. No legislative act therefore contrary to the Constitution, can be valid. To deny this would be to affirm that the deputy is greater than his principal; that the servant is above his master; that the representatives of the people are superior to the people themselves; that men acting by virtue of powers may do not only what their powers do not authorise, but what they forbid.

If it be said that the legislative body are themselves the constitutional judges of their own powers, and that the construction they put upon them is conclusive upon the other departments, it may be answered, that this cannot be the natural presumption, where it is not to be collected from any particular provisions in the Constitution. It is not otherwise to be supposed that the Constitution could intend to enable the representatives of the people to substitute their *will* to that of their constituents. It is far more rational to suppose that the courts were designed to be an intermediate body between the people and the legislature, in order, among other things, to keep the latter within the limits assigned to their authority. The interpretation of the laws is the proper and peculiar province of the courts. A constitution is in fact, and must be, regarded by the judges as a fundamental law. It therefore belongs to them to ascertain its meaning as well as the meaning of any particular act proceeding from the legislative body. If there should happen to be an irreconcilable variance between the two, that which has the superior obligation and validity ought of course to be preferred; or in other words, the Constitution ought to be preferred to the statute, the intention of the people to the intention of their agents.

Nor does this conclusion by any means suppose a superiority of the judicial to the legislative power. It only supposes that the power of the people is superior to both; and that where the will of the legislature declared in its statutes, stands in opposition to that of the people declared in the Constitution, the judges ought to be governed by the latter rather than the former. They ought to regulate their decisions by the fundamental laws, rather than by those which are not fundamental. . . .

If then the courts of justice are to be considered the bulwarks of a limited constitution against legislative encroachments, this consideration will afford a strong argument for the permanent tenure of judicial offices, since nothing will contribute to much as this to that independent spirit in the judges, which must be essential to the faithful performance of so arduous a duty. . . .

That inflexible and uniform adherence to the rights of the Constitution and of individuals, which we perceive to be indispensable in the courts of justice, can certainly not be expected from judges who hold their offices by a temporary commission. Periodical appointments, however regulated, or by whomsoever made, would in some way or other be fatal to their necessary independence. If the power of making them was committed either to the executive or legislature, there would be danger of an improper complaisance to the branch which possessed it; if to both, there would be an unwillingness to hazard the displeasure of either; if to the people, or to persons chosen by them for the special purpose, there would be too great a disposition to consult popularity, to justify a reliance that nothing would be consulted but the Constitution and the laws.

There is yet a further and a weighty reason for the permanency of the judicial offices; which is deducible from the nature of the qualifications they require. It has been frequently remarked with great propriety, that a voluminous code of laws is one of the inconveniences necessarily connected with the advantages of a free government. To avoid an arbitrary discretion in the courts, it is indispensable that they should be bound down by strict rules and precedents, which serve to define and point out their duty in every particular case that comes before them; and it will readily be conceived from the variety of controversies which grow out of the folly and wickedness of mankind, that the records of those precedents must unavoidably swell to a very considerable bulk, and must demand long and laborious study to acquire a competent knowledge of them. Hence it is that there can be but few men in the society, who will have sufficient skill in the laws to qualify them for the stations of judges. And making the proper deductions for the ordinary depravity of human nature, the number must be still smaller of those who unite the requisite integrity with the requisite knowledge. These considerations apprise us, that the government can have no great option between fit characters; and that a temporary duration in office, which would naturally discourage such characters from quitting a lucrative line of practice to accept a seat on the bench, would have a tendency to throw the administration of justice into hands less able, and less well qualified to conduct it with utility and dignity. In the present circumstances of this country, and in those in which it is likely to be for a long time to come, the disadvantages on this score would be greater than they may at first sight appear; but it must be confessed that they are far inferior to those which present themselves under the other aspects of the subject.

Upon the whole there can be no room to doubt that the convention acted wisely in copying from the models of those constitutions which have established *good behaviour* as the tenure of their judicial offices in point of duration; and that so far from being blamable on this account, their plan would have been inexcusably defective if it had wanted this important feature of good government. The experience of Great Britain affords an illustrious comment on the excellence of the institution.

PUBLIUS

CHAPTER ONE

THE REVOLUTIONARY ORIGINS OF THE AMERICAN CONSTITUTION

AMERICA'S CONSTITUTIONAL HISTORY did not begin in 1787 with those Founding Fathers who gathered in Philadelphia, in the building we now call Independence Hall. Indeed, it did not begin with America's Declaration of Independence, adopted in that same building on July 4, 1776. Rather, it developed gradually over the nearly two hundred years of British rule preceding America's bold leap toward independence.

America's legal and constitutional traditions were influenced profoundly by English common law and by a deep reverence for what British subjects on both sides of the Atlantic called the "English constitution." It did not seem to matter that the English constitution did not actually exist in written form—it was and is a jumble of parliamentary statute, legal precedent, and simple custom. Yet English colonizers and American colonists alike held it in uncommonly high regard.

It was in large measure the disagreements between Americans and Englishmen over how to interpret the English constitution that precipitated the conflict that would result in the world's first popular revolution. The origins of the conflict lay in two things that have caused trouble since the beginning of time: money and taxes. In 1763 the British government, following a successful but costly war against France (as well as against some of France's Indian allies in North America), found itself in possession of vast amounts of new territory west of the Appalachian Mountains and in Canada. That was the good news. The bad news was that the costs of the war, and the likely continuing costs of protecting the newly won gains, had left the king and his government deeply in debt, with the prospect of even greater debt on the horizon. Since much of that debt had been incurred in a war fought in America and since the spoils of that war—vast lands stretching west to the Mississippi River and north into Canada—would ultimately be sources of opportunity for future generations of American colonists, from the British point of view it seemed only reasonable that Americans pay their fair share of the costs.

Of course, the Americans saw things differently. They too had sacrificed. They had provided supplies and, more important, militiamen who had fought alongside the British regular army during that seven-year-long war. Indeed, a young colonel in the Virginia militia, George Washington, had acquired an international reputation for his bravery as commander of the Virginia regiment in the French and Indian War. If there was ever a time in which Americans were in a mood to be left alone to enjoy the relative peace of a world in which the threat of French intrigue and Indian warfare on their frontiers was significantly diminished, that time came at the conclusion of the war, signaled by the signing of the Treaty of Paris in February 1763. At precisely the moment when the British government was looking to America for an unprecedented contribution to the British treasury, for "the good of the empire," Americans, weary of sacrifice and less dependent on British military might for the security of their frontiers than ever before, were in an entirely different frame of mind.

Beginning in 1764 and 1765 the British parliament began levying a new series of taxes on the colonies aimed at raising revenue to pay the expenses of administering their empire. The British government also announced its intention to tighten up enforcement of existing customs laws, which, because of lax enforcement over many decades, had been widely evaded by American merchants. In fact, the taxes imposed on the colonies—a tax on molasses imported from the West Indies into America and a stamp tax, similar to taxes already levied back in England—did not present a major economic burden to the Americans. But the means by which the taxes were imposed—enacted by a distant Parliament without the Americans' consent—seemed to the Americans to violate a principle of the English constitution that they valued dearly: the principle of "no taxation without representation."

The American protests against the taxes began in the colonies' provincial assemblies, which sent humble petitions to Parliament asking for a repeal of what they believed to be unjust and unconstitutional acts. But protest was not confined to humble petitions. Gradually, ordinary folks in America's cities and towns joined the protests, and as American resistance assumed this popular dimension, the forms of protest—street marches and demonstrations; economic boycotts of British goods; and, at times, violence aimed at British officials charged with enforcing the acts— became more direct and more threatening to the authority of the Crown. What began as a constitutional debate between American and English political leaders was becoming something more explosive—an intensely personal conflict between British officials and ordinary Americans played out, not in legislatures or courtrooms, but in the streets of Boston, New York, and Philadelphia.

Resistance bred reaction, and the British responded by sending more troops to keep order in their restive colonies. Parliament was goaded into passing additional legislation—not simply taxes but other measures, such as those requiring Americans to provide lodging for British troops in their homes—further inflaming public opinion. The turning point in the escalating conflict between the Crown and colonies came on a cold, moonlit night on December 16, 1773. Earlier in the year, Parliament had passed the Tea Act, a law not only intended to reassert England's right to tax the colonies but which also gave the East India Company—the company that enjoyed a monopoly on all English trade in India—a similar monopoly on all tea imported into America. Once again the amount of the tax involved was relatively trivial, but Americans now rose up in protest, not only against being taxed without their consent, but also against the threat of monopoly. If Parliament could give one company a monopoly on the importation of tea, what was to prevent it from doing the same with other commodities, leaving American merchants, and all those who worked for them, out in the cold?

So on that cold night in December, three small groups of men poorly disguised as Mohawk Indians—but who were in fact common seamen and urban laborers acting under the direction of the political activist Samuel Adams—dumped ninety thousand pounds of East India Company tea into Boston Harbor. John Adams, a witness to the event, wrote in his diary that night that "this destruction of the tea is so bold, so daring, so firm, intrepid and inflexible, and it must have so important Consequences, and so lasting, that I cannot but consider it an Epocha in History." Indeed, the effects of the Boston mob action would shake politicians in England to their very core, setting in motion a chain of events that would change the world.

⚜

SOME IN AMERICA REGRETTED THE PROVOCATIVE MANNER in which the Bostonians had acted, but when the British parliament responded with a harsh set of measures aimed at punishing the colony of Massachusetts, public opinion began to change. The Coercive Acts, as they came to be called, not only closed the port of Boston, but also strengthened the power of the royal governor while dissolving the provincial legislature and restricting the actions of town meetings. This aggressive display of parliamentary power posed an obvious threat not merely to Massachusetts, but to the liberties of all Americans. The constitutional battlefield had now expanded: the issues now confronting Americans went beyond taxation to the wider question of whether Parliament had any political authority over the American colonies. In June of 1774, all thirteen of America's provincial legislatures, accustomed to going their separate ways, agreed to send delegates to Philadelphia to meet in a Continental Congress in order to work out a common response to this new and dangerous provocation.

When the delegates gathered in a carpenters' guild hall in Philadelphia on September 5, 1774, there was general agreement among them that some response to the Coercive Acts was necessary but little consensus on what that response should be. For a few—particularly those like John and Samuel Adams from fractious Boston and the Virginian Patrick Henry—the idea of independence was beginning to seem like a possible, even desirable, outcome. But most of the delegates to the Continental Congress retained a deep affection for their monarch and for the English constitution. Surely, there must be some means of resolving the conflict short of revolution. The magnitude of the change being proposed by the advocates of independence—a revolution in which Americans would be transformed from loyal subjects of a beloved British king into independent citizens in a new republic—was almost too much to comprehend. Yet gradually, haltingly, America's political leaders, and the constituents they represented, would set themselves on a course to independence—to a rejection of their identity as British *subjects* and a declaration of their desire to be *citizens* of the "united states."

The Continental Congress met in Philadelphia's Carpenters' Hall between September 5 and October 26, 1774, and after a six-month recess moved to the Assembly Room of the Pennsylvania State House, the building that would later be called Independence Hall. They met continuously from May 10, 1775, until the adoption of the Declaration of Independence on July 4, 1776. From May 1775 forward, the constitutional battle was waged on two fronts: between political leaders in America and their counterparts in London, and among the American delegates to the Continental Congress, who continued to disagree about whether independence was the course for the colonies to take. The latter debate was profoundly influenced by the steadily escalating conflict between Great Britain and the colonies outside the halls of Congress and, just as importantly, by the climate of opinion back home in the delegates' respective colonies.

The battles of Lexington and Concord, occurring less than a month before the Continental Congress reconvened in May 1775, provided one flash point, transforming the conflict between Crown and colonies from a political dispute to a military confrontation. But even after the opposing patriot and British armies had taken up arms, most Americans hoped for a solution that would not force them to abandon their loyalties as British subjects. As the skirmishes at Lexington and Concord escalated into full-scale war—Bunker Hill in June 1775, military clashes spreading to a new front in western New York and Quebec in the fall of 1775, Virginia royal governor Lord Dunmore's promise of freedom to slaves who deserted their masters and fought on the British side to put down incipient rebellion in that colony—it became more and more difficult to imagine a path toward reconciliation.

Still the delegates sought that reconciliation. John Dickinson, a delegate to the Continental Congress from Pennsylvania, had already made a name for himself in the preceding years as an articulate spokesman for the constitutional rights of Americans. But Dickinson, trained as a lawyer in London, also had a deep reverence for the English constitution. *If only* the king and Parliament could be persuaded to return to the true principles of that constitution and to restore their liberties! In August 1775 Dickinson persuaded the Congress to draft the Olive Branch Petition, which firmly reiterated the Americans' constitutional objections to Parliament's attempts to tax and legislate for the colonies but at the same time expressed affection for and allegiance to the British Empire. Notably, the petition was sent, not to Parliament, but to King George III, for even moderate Americans like Dickinson had reached the point of denying all parliamentary authority over the colonies.

⊙∰〜

WHATEVER HOPES OF ENLISTING THE AID OF their sovereign that men like Dickinson may have entertained, they were coldly dashed by late October 1775, when the Congress received news that the king had declared the colonies in a state of rebellion even before receiving the Olive Branch Petition. When the petition finally reached the king, he refused to look at it. To make matters worse, in his October speech at the opening of Parliament (which the Continental Congress only learned about in early January 1776), George III denounced the Congress as "promoters of [a] desperate conspiracy." Its petitions, he charged, were only a ruse designed to lull the British while the delegates were preparing for a "general revolt," with the ultimate goal being the establishment of "an independent empire." And although the news would not reach America until the end of February, Parliament, at the king's urging, had passed the Prohibitory Act, which effectively declared war on American commerce on the high seas. With the adamant refusal of the king to help turn the tide of events back toward reconciliation, the next move would be up to the Americans.

At nearly the same time that George III was making pronouncements that dimmed the hopes of those in Congress who yearned for some sort of honorable path toward reconciliation, a scruffy, recent English immigrant to Pennsylvania, one Thomas Paine, wrote a pamphlet, *Common Sense*, that would bring about a revolution in public opinion. Paine had nothing but contempt for the "boasted constitution of England," which was, he derisively commented, "noble for the dark and slavish times in which it was erected," but wholly inadequate for a free people in a new world. And the greatest absurdity of that constitution, he exclaimed, was the very idea of a hereditary monarch. His attack on the monarchy in general, and on George III in particular, was devastating and, as it turned out, unanswerable. John Dickinson, whose devotion to the English constitution formed the core of his desire to stay within the British Empire, was rendered mute in the face of Paine's assault. And General George Washington, now leading the Continental army's troops in battle, was so moved by Paine's pamphlet that he had his officers read it to his men in the field to inspire them to fight for the common cause.

The period between the publication of *Common Sense* in mid-January and the decision to declare independence in early July was a chaotic one. At this stage the decision on independence became not one but thirteen separate decisions, as political leaders and ordinary citizens in each of the colonies read and then debated the argument in *Common Sense*. In Congress, those continuing to hope for reconciliation found their numbers declining and their arguments less persuasive. Nevertheless, even those delegates most committed to independence knew that the drama needed to be played out in each of the individual colonies, for the authority of the Congress was ultimately dependent on public opinion beyond the walls of the Pennsylvania State House.

By April of 1776, most, but by no means a decisive majority, of the colonies appeared ready to declare independence. A few—Pennsylvania, New York, Maryland, and New Jersey—had, with varying degrees of emphasis, instructed their delegates to the Congress to *oppose* any resolution for independence. But as the possibilities for reconciliation with Great Britain dwindled (the British government had indicated that it might send peace commissioners to America to attempt to negotiate a settlement, but the commissioners never arrived), those colonies that had argued for caution were left with few plausible alternatives.

On June 7, Richard Henry Lee of Virginia introduced into the Congress a resolution sent to him by a specially called convention in his home colony. The resolution proposed:

- that these United Colonies are, and of right ought to be free and independent states.
- that it is expedient forthwith to take the most effectual measures for forming foreign alliances.
- that a plan of confederation be prepared and transmitted to the respective Colonies for their consideration and approbation.

Agreement on these three items—independence; foreign assistance; and, perhaps most important, union—constituted the essential preconditions for a formal declaration of independence.

Even with those resolutions before the Congress, the delegates from Pennsylvania, New York, New Jersey, and Maryland remained opposed, and others seemed to be on the fence. As a consequence, the Congress postponed debate on the resolutions from Virginia until July 1. But on that day, as debate on the resolutions began, nearly everyone gathered in the Assembly Room of the Pennsylvania State House knew that they had reached a moment of truth. During the first go-around, on July 1, Pennsylvania and South Carolina opposed the resolution for independence, with Delaware divided. And New York's delegates had to sit on their hands, for they had been given explicit instructions by their legislature *not* to vote on any measure aimed at independence.

Finally, on July 2 the votes fell into place. An additional Delaware delegate, Caesar Rodney, arrived in Philadelphia that day, voting in favor of independence and breaking the deadlock in that delegation. Edward Rutledge of South Carolina, who had opposed independence, deferred to his older, more politically powerful brother, John Rutledge, and agreed to support the resolutions. The situation with the Pennsylvania delegation was the most interesting. Although prominent Pennsylvania delegates like John Dickinson and Robert Morris continued to oppose independence, they realized that their views were out of step with those of their constituents. Recognizing that their duty to their constituents was more important than their personal feelings, they voluntarily absented themselves from the voting on Richard Henry Lee's resolution for independence on July 2. The effect of their absence was to tip the balance within the Pennsylvania delegation toward independence. The

New Yorkers still sat on their hands, waiting for their legislature to have a change of heart. But at least they had not voted no, allowing John Adams to crow that the "resolution was passed without one dissenting colony." The following day he wrote his wife, Abigail, in exultation: "the second day of July, 1776 will be the most memorable epocha in the history of America. I am apt to believe that it will be celebrated by succeeding generations as the great anniversary Festival." He missed the mark by two days.

The man most closely associated with American independence has turned out not to be its most indefatigable advocate, John Adams, but rather a relative newcomer to the political scene: the soft-spoken, lanky Virginian Thomas Jefferson. On June 11, three weeks before the formal vote on independence, the Continental Congress had appointed a committee composed of Jefferson, Adams, Benjamin Franklin, Roger Sherman, and Robert Livingston to prepare a declaration of independence, in case such a declaration should be necessary.

It was of course Jefferson who took on the task of completing a first draft of the Declaration of Independence. But if we are to believe the testimony of John Adams, that was not a foregone conclusion. According to Adams, when the committee first met it decided that Jefferson would be given that task, but Jefferson proposed instead that Adams do it. Then followed an exchange in which each man tried to persuade the other to write the draft. Adams argued that Jefferson should do it because he was a Virginian, "and a Virginian ought to appear at the head of this business," a reference to the fact that New Englanders like Adams were seen by many as the troublemakers who had gotten the colonies into the conflict with England in the first place, and that it would look better if the more conservative Virginians took the lead in the movement for independence. Adams went on to say that "I am obnoxious, suspected, and unpopular. You are very much otherwise." That, unfortunately, was probably true, for Adams's curmudgeonly nature, together with his often abrasive insistence on independence even before some of the other colonies were ready for it, had earned him at least a few enemies. Adams's third reason was that he believed Jefferson could "write ten times better than I can." It is hard to imagine Adams admitting that anyone was a better writer, and indeed Jefferson— again, long after the fact—had a rather different recollection. According to Jefferson, the decision about who was to write the draft of the Declaration was straightforward: the members of the committee "unanimously pressed on myself alone to undertake the draught [and] I consented." Jefferson went on to recall that at that point he retired to his rented rooms at Seventh and Market Streets in Philadelphia and wrote a draft, and before sending it formally to the committee for their comments, he informally asked both Benjamin Franklin and John Adams to suggest corrections. According to Jefferson, "their alterations were two or three only, and merely verbal." At which point, Jefferson recalled, he wrote out a new copy of the document and reported it to the committee, which, without making alterations, sent it to the full Congress for its consideration.

In fact, the rough draft of Jefferson's Declaration that was submitted to the Congress had a total of twenty-six alterations—two in Adams's handwriting, five in Franklin's, and sixteen in Jefferson's. And three additional paragraphs were added as well. It appears likely that many of the changes were the result of further conversations that Jefferson had with Adams and Franklin, both of whom made substantial contributions to the revisions of Jefferson's original draft. When comparing the two drafts, it is sometimes difficult to tell whether the revisions were made by Jefferson or made by others but recorded in Jefferson's handwriting, but there is no doubt that the revisions did make the document both more elegant and more forceful. To give just a few examples:

1. The initial draft stated: "We hold these truths to be self-evident: that all men are created equal & independent; that from that equal creation they derive rights inherent & inalienable, among which are the preservation of life, & liberty, & the pursuit of happiness."

   > The final draft: "We hold these truths to be self-evident, that all men are created equal, that they are endowed by their Creator with certain unalienable Rights, that among these are Life, Liberty, and the pursuit of Happiness."

2. The concluding portion of the preamble initially read: "The history of his present majesty is a history of unremitting injuries and usurpations, among which no one fact stands single or solitary to contradict the uniform tenor of the rest, all of which have in direct object the establishment of an absolute tyranny over these states. [T]o prove this, let facts be submitted to a candid world, for the truth of which we pledge a faith yet unsullied by falsehood."

   > This was shortened to read: "The history of the present King of Great Britain is a history of repeated injuries and usurpations, all having in direct object the establishment of an absolute tyranny over these States. To prove this, let Facts be submitted to a candid world."

Both of these sets of changes made the document both more concise and elegant, and by doing so, more powerful.

The list of grievances that followed was anything but a fair-minded and evenhanded assessment of the conflict between Great Britain and America. Rather, it was aimed at persuading those Americans who remained undecided to support the patriot cause and, equally important, at signaling to potential European allies, particularly France, that America was serious about its intent to break with England—an action that, if successful, would significantly weaken the British Empire in North America.

Although the Declaration was adopted on July 4, the only two members of the Continental Congress who appear to have signed it on that day were John Hancock, the Congress's president, and Charles Thomson, the Congress's secretary. The final wording of the Declaration was apparently engrossed on parchment sometime between July 19 and August 2. On the latter date, some but not all members of the Congress signed it, with those members who were absent on August 2 trickling in to sign it in subsequent days. Although some of the reasons for the delay were purely logistical—the members of the Congress first needed to get the document properly engrossed on parchment, and then they had to round up those delegates who were prepared to sign it—another was more substantial. The Declaration begins with the words: "The unanimous Declaration of the thirteen united States of America." The New York legislature did not give its delegates permission to support independence until July 9, and if the Declaration was truly to be a unanimous one, the members of the Congress had to be sure that New York was on board.

Whatever the delay in signing the document, there was little delay in proclaiming it to a vitally interested public. When John Hancock transmitted America's Declaration to the states on July 6, he observed: "The important consequences . . . from this Declaration of Independence, considered as the Ground and Foundation of a future Government will naturally suggest the Propriety of proclaiming it in such a Manner, that the People may be universally informed of it." In fact, someone had gotten hold of a copy of the Declaration a day earlier, and on July 5 a group of citizens gathered in the yard of the Independence Hall and listened as America's first founding document was read aloud. Three days later there was another, "official" reading of the Declaration in that same spot, and within a few days similar readings occurred in the principal public gathering places all over America. General George Washington, already fully engaged in battle against the British army, ordered his officers in New York City to read copies of the Declaration to their troops, and with their British adversaries "constantly in view," the troops were "formed in hollow squares on their respective parades," and the Declaration was read "with an audible voice." Washington hoped that these public—even daring—readings would "serve as a free incentive to every officer, and soldier, to act with Fidelity and Courage . . . knowing that now the peace and safety of his Country depends (under God) solely on the success of our arms."

America's political leaders in the Continental Congress, and American soldiers in the field, had taken the bold, fateful step of *declaring* their independence from Great Britain. But the struggle to *achieve* independence would sorely test the will of all Americans.

CHAPTER TWO

AMERICA STRUGGLES TO ACHIEVE INDEPENDENCE, LIBERTY, AND UNION

GOVERNMENT UNDER THE ARTICLES OF CONFEDERATION

JEFFERSON'S DECLARATION WAS a bold, inspiring piece of prose. But what did it really mean? By what means would Americans achieve the independence they had proclaimed? And, equally important, how would they put into practice the lofty ideals that had served as their rationale for independence? Jefferson and his fellow Americans had set for themselves the formidable task not only of winning independence by force of arms against the world's greatest military power but also of remaining true to the principles that had motivated their epochal decision to seek independence. The most formidable challenge—one that would persist for many decades after independence was achieved—was that of bringing the reality of social, economic, and political arrangements within the independent American states into harmony with the promise contained in Jefferson's preamble: "We hold these truths to be self-evident, that all men are created equal, that they are endowed by their Creator with certain unalienable Rights, that among these are Life, Liberty, and the pursuit of Happiness." Those hopeful phrases would prove a powerful inspiration for Americans for many generations to come, but the precise meaning of those words remains a subject of immense dispute among Americans right up to the present day.

Americans had made substantial progress toward meeting the promise of equality and of the "pursuit of Happiness" during the years since the founding of their colonies. In 1630 John Winthrop, the governor of the newly created Massachusetts Bay colony, lectured the first settlers of that colony, as they made their way to America aboard the ship *Arbella*, that "God Almighty in his most holy and wise Providence hath soe disposed of the condition of mankind as in all times some must be rich, some poore, some high and eminent in power and dignitie, others mean and in subjection." In Winthrop's view, inequality was not merely the natural state of mankind but, indeed, a divinely ordained one. Much would happen in America between 1630 and 1776 to undermine that hierarchical formula for the proper ordering of society. The combined influence of European Enlightenment ideas and the economic opportunity offered by the bountiful American landscape would bring to England's American subjects a greater degree of prosperity, liberty, and personal independence than any of the original colonizers of America ever could have imagined. Yet in a whole range of categories—the institution of African slavery; the relationship between Europeans and Indians in America; the systematic legal subordination of women; and indeed the significant social and legal distinctions existing even among free white men—Americans in 1776 had only barely begun to recognize the logical imperatives of Jefferson's lofty phrases.

Thomas Paine, in urging Americans to make the fateful commitment to independence, had held out the promise that:

We have it in our power to begin the world over again. A situation similar to the present has not happened since the days of Noah until now. The birthday of a new world is at hand, and a race of men, perhaps as numerous as all Europe contains, are to receive their portion of freedom from the events of a few months.

"To begin the world over again," with new forms of government and habits of freedom that would extend the principles of liberty across all of America—what a remarkable opportunity! And as the former British colonies began to create governments as independent states, they took a few tentative steps in that direction. Perhaps the most immediate, and revolutionary, change occurred in the way in which Americans conceived themselves. John Adams, observing the events surrounding independence, remarked:

Is not the change we have seen astonishing? Would any Man, two years ago, have believed it possible to accomplish such an Alteration in the Prejudices, Passions, Sentiments of these thirteen little States to make every one of them completely republican . . . ? Idolatry to Monarchs, and servility to Aristocratical Pride was never so totally eradicated from so Many Minds in so short a time.

In what seemed like a heartbeat, Americans cast aside their only previous source of common identity—as subjects of an English king—and embraced a new identity as "citizens." As a South Carolina physician, David Ramsay, analyzed it, the change "from subjects to citizens" was immense: "Subjects look up to a master, but citizens are so far equal, that none have hereditary rights superior to others. Each citizen of a free state contains, within himself, by nature and the constitution, as much of the common sovereignty as another."

"By nature and the constitution"—but what was a constitution? The other vitally important thing that Americans came to recognize in the aftermath of their struggle with the English king and parliament was that the English constitution—an unwritten hodgepodge of statutory law, legal precedent, and custom—was not an adequate safeguard of a people's liberties. As the newly independent American states began to create their own governments, they came to realize that *written* constitutions, explicit both in the powers they delegated to the government and the fundamental rights that all citizens were to enjoy, were the only secure means of protecting liberty and promoting the public good.

As they crafted their revolutionary state constitutions, America's political leaders, most of them born to positions of privilege and carrying within them a residual affection for the ways of the traditional order, made some forward strides in recognizing the promise contained in Paine's optimistic call to "begin the world over again." Most states included in their new constitutions bills of rights specifically spelling out those "unalienable Rights" to which Jefferson had referred in the Declaration of Independence. Some states passed laws making it easier for free white males to vote. Most states, however, retained at least some form of property qualification for voting. With the threat of monarchical tyranny still fresh in their minds, most state constitutions moved to weaken the executive branch and to strengthen the lower houses of assembly, the one branch of government whose authority derived most directly from the people. With the expansion of the powers of the state legislatures, most states increased the number of representatives serving in those legislatures. And the characteristics of those serving in the legislatures began to change as well; although public service in high office continued for the most part to be the preserve of the wealthy and wellborn, it became more common for men of moderate wealth and social status to be elected to public office as well.

America did not, however, become an egalitarian society overnight. The institution of chattel slavery continued to be entrenched in the independent southern states. Women, free blacks, and white males who did not own property continued to face legal impediments to full citizenship. And the combination of ethnic hostility and hunger for western lands caused Euro-Americans to continue their warfare against American Indian cultures. In all of these senses, the American Revolution fell short of the promise of equality contained in the Declaration of Independence. The American Revolution was, at least by the terms of the challenge that Thomas Paine had issued in *Common Sense*, an unfinished one.

America has struggled to fulfill the commitments to democracy, equality, and liberty made in the Declaration of Independence for all its history, but the struggle for independence presented another challenge as well: how should Americans proceed in organizing a union among the American states? In answering that essential question, the Americans faced a troublesome dilemma. On the one hand, one of the central causes of the American Revolution was the justifiable fear of an overly centralized government imposing its will from afar. Certainly among the logical conclusions to be drawn from the struggles against British rule leading up to independence were that it was necessary to keep government small; to keep it weak; and, most importantly, to locate that government physically close to the people, so those exercising political power could be closely watched. Yet the imperatives of fighting and winning a war against one of the world's most formidable military powers demanded that the thirteen colonies, each of which had in the past enjoyed closer ties and more cordial relations with the imperial government in London than they had with one another, called for an energetic government with the power to compel the states to cooperate in the common cause. It was one thing to *declare* independence; it was quite another to *secure* it. The success of the military aspect of the Revolution required the mobilization of an army drawn from all the colonies; the battles of that Revolution crossed state boundaries; and, most important, the financing of the war required a degree of sacrifice among Americans, in the name not of any individual state but of the "united States," far greater than anything the British had ever demanded of them. How would the former British colonies in America, unused to any form of continental union and indeed often ignorant and suspicious of one another, reconcile their desires for local autonomy with the demands of their drastically changed circumstances?

America's patriot leaders knew that some form of central government was necessary if they were to achieve their independence. Indeed, the resolution proposing independence first introduced into the Second Continental Congress by Richard Henry Lee on June 7, 1776, explicitly presented the notion of an intercolonial *union* as a necessary accompaniment to independence. But what form would that union take?

The general outlines of a plan of union began to be considered as early as June 11, 1776, before the Declaration of Independence had even been adopted. At that time the Continental Congress appointed a committee, chaired by John Dickinson of Pennsylvania, to draft a "plan of confederation." Dickinson's initial draft of that plan was a bold one. It acknowledged that the newly created states should have control over their "present Laws, Customs, Rights, Privileges, and peculiar Jurisdictions," but it then added the important proviso that the states' law-making powers "shall not interfere with the Articles of this Confederation." Equally important, Dickinson's draft gave to the proposed confederation's government the exclusive power of "Settling all Disputes and Differences" between or among the former colonies. And, in what would prove to be its most contentious feature, the draft also gave the confederation's Congress the power to make all decisions relating to the disposition of any western lands secured during the Revolution.

Debate on Dickinson's draft of the Articles of Confederation unfolded sporadically in the Continental Congress between July 1776 and October 1777. Many of the powers that Dickinson proposed to give to the central government were stripped away by delegates fearful that their states were giving up too much of their own power. The resulting Articles of Confederation and Perpetual Union was not really a proper constitution but, rather, a peace treaty among the thirteen separate states. It amounted to little more than a "league of friendship," a form of alliance in which "each state retains its sovereignty, freedom, and independence, and every power, jurisdiction, and right, which is not by this Confederation expressly delegated to the United States, in Congress assembled." Although it gave the proposed government enormous responsibility—to provide for the states' "common defence, the security of their liberties and their mutual and general welfare"—it denied that government most of the powers necessary to carry out those responsibilities. The Confederation government lacked the power to tax; it could only "request" voluntary contributions of money from the independent states in order to support the war effort. It lacked the power to regulate commerce among the states—an omission that sometimes caused the states to behave more like quarreling nations than members of a single nation. The Articles of Confederation also failed to provide for a chief executive capable of giving energy and focus to the new government. The representatives in the only functioning branch of the government, the Continental Congress, took their orders from their state legislatures, with one of the consequences being that apathy within the Congress was so great that it would sometimes go for weeks, even months, without meeting.

The proposed Articles of Confederation were submitted to the individual state legislatures for their approval in November 1777; it took another three and a half years, until March 1781, before the proposal received the necessary unanimous approval from all thirteen states—yet another indication of the inclination of the states to jealously guard their sovereignty and to zealously protect their provincial interests, often at the expense of the good of the aspiring nation as a whole.

In the meantime, General George Washington, commander in chief of the Continental army, as well as the civilian leaders in the Continental Congress, were left to fight a war and attempt to hold an informal union of the states together without an officially sanctioned frame of government. The task of fighting and winning a war against Great Britain would have been daunting in any circumstance, but armed with the power only to "request" contributions of men, matériel, and money from the individual states, General Washington's job was made even more difficult. The war effort during those early years was as successful as it was in part because of Washington's leadership, but also—and equally important—because of the bravery and self-sacrifice of those among his men who, even when the terms of their enlistments were up, stayed to fight on. It benefited as well from the lack of decisiveness of the British army—an army hampered both by a long line of supply, stretching across the Atlantic Ocean, and a hesitant ministry back at home, which on the one hand wished to put down the colonial revolt but on the other was reluctant to make the sort of full-fledged military and naval commitment that would have brought the rebellious colonies to heel.

America's commitment to liberty and independence was accompanied by a surge of utopian idealism in 1776, with the state governments enthusiastically pledging to contribute to the common cause. But as the optimism of 1776 confronted the reality of a bloody and protracted war, officials in the Continental government found it increasingly difficult to persuade the states to live up to their obligations.

America's eventual victory over the British, who surrendered at Yorktown, Virginia, in October 1781, seemed nearly miraculous; it owed as much to timely French military aid and English indecision as to America's military prowess. And even after victory had been achieved and the American union under the Articles of Confederation received official sanction from all thirteen states, the task of holding that fragile union of states together proved formidable. It was a task made more difficult still by the fact that the new Continental government had accumulated a substantial debt both to private individuals and foreign nations in the course of the Revolutionary War. Once the war was over and peace had returned, the state governments were even less interested in contributing their fair share to help the Continental government meet its obligations. By 1785 and 1786, with France and Holland clamoring for repayment of the monies owed them, the financial condition of the young American republic seemed even more perilous.

Nor was the weakness of the central government the only problem. Many of the men who made the journey to Philadelphia in 1787 also believed that the revolutionary state constitutions were seriously defective. Those state constitutions were noble experiments; indeed they were the world's first *written* constitutions. But they seemed to many to have given the popularly elected legislatures of the states excessive power at the expense of the executive branch of government. Many of the members of those state legislatures had pursued policies which, though popular in the eyes of the people who elected them, served to undermine the financial stability of the young republic and, in a few cases, the public order as well.

Fears about the weakness and irresponsibility of the state governments were given frightening expression when, in the late fall of 1786, a discontented group of western Massachusetts farmers, including one Daniel Shays—after whom the uprising came to be named—took up arms in rebellion against the policies of the Massachusetts state government. Although Shays' Rebellion was quickly put down, men like Virginia's James Madison and George Washington began to worry that the very fabric of government and society was beginning to tear, and as they watched a somnolent Continental Congress that seemed powerless to accomplish much of anything, that worry turned to despair. General Washington, upon receiving a letter from his friend and neighbor Henry Lee asking him to use his "influence" to set things in the country right, exploded in frustration: "You talk, my good Sir, of employing influence. . . . Influence is no government. . . . Let the reins of government be braced and then held with a steady hand, and every violation of the Constitution be reprehended: if defective, let it be amended, but not suffered to be trampled upon whilst it has an existence."

Most Americans at that time were too preoccupied with their own lives to worry either about the weaknesses of the Continental government or about an unsuccessful uprising of farmers in Massachusetts; but for those who worried about the fate of America, not as a loose collection of states but rather as a single nation, those developments seemed profoundly troubling. In 1776 most Americans believed that the greatest threat to liberty was to be found in the overriding power of a distant, centralized government. But the men who provided the energy and intellect behind the movement for a new constitution—their hopes and fears shaped by the challenges and frustrations of fighting a long, costly war and of securing peace and public order at home—had come to believe that the lack of "energy" in the Continental government posed an equally formidable threat to liberty. As they prepared to meet in the Pennsylvania State House—the same building in which Americans had declared their independence in 1776—they were in a mood to launch a second revolution in American government.

CHAPTER THREE

THE CONSTITUTIONAL CONVENTION OF 1787

A REVOLUTION IN GOVERNMENT

THE FIFTY-FIVE MEN WHO GATHERED in the Assembly Room of the Pennsylvania State House in the summer of 1787 faced a formidable task. The thirteen "united states" that comprised the American union under the Articles of Confederation were in fact profoundly *disunited*. America, by the extraordinary expanse of its territory, the ethnic and religious diversity of its population, and the existence of thirteen independent and sovereign states, each possessing distinct cultural and political traditions and a multitude of varying and competing interests, was by no means inevitably meant to be a single nation.

As things have turned out, the framers of the Constitution were remarkably successful in their enterprise. The Constitution they drafted has proven a remarkable achievement: It is the world's oldest written national constitution. It has, for the most part, been successful in striking that difficult balance between the maintenance of public order and security, on the one hand, and the nurturing and protection of personal liberty, on the other. And it has brought remarkable stability to one of the most tumultuous forms of political activity: popular democracy.

But it didn't begin that way, nor was the outcome of the

Constitutional Convention in any way inevitable. As we look at the work of the Founding Fathers during that summer of 1787, it seems a wonder that things turned out as well as they did.

As the framers of the Constitution set about their work, they were confronted by a vexing dilemma. The central unifying idea behind America's rejection of British monarchical rule in 1776 was the belief that governmental power was inherently aggressive, inherently dangerous. The best way to protect liberty, the revolutionaries of 1776 believed, was to keep government relatively weak and keep it close to the people, where those entrusted with power could be closely watched. The very last thing that they wished to do was create a strong central government, distant and isolated from the people of the country. Yet, as we have seen, America's patriot leaders knew some form of central government was necessary to fight and win a war against one of the world's great military powers and thus achieve their quest for independence. The first logical—if inadequate—step in creating a workable union among the states was the government under the Articles of Confederation. As the year 1786 drew to a close, with the Continental government facing bankruptcy and with armed insurrection threatening peace and public order in Massachusetts, those political leaders who had led America's fight for independence began to realize that dramatic action needed to be taken if they were going to preserve the very aim of their quest: the preservation of both *liberty* and *order*.

THE ANNAPOLIS CONVENTION

These crises in government coincided with the convening of a small group of delegates in Annapolis, Maryland, on September 11, 1786, to discuss a more "uniform system" of commercial relations among the states. The so-called Annapolis Convention was a strictly extralegal gathering and, in truth, it failed altogether to achieve its stated mission. Only twelve delegates, from five of the thirteen states, turned up, and, lacking a quorum, there was not really much that they could accomplish. But those twelve delegates who went to the trouble to make the trip to Annapolis—among them John Dickinson, Alexander Hamilton, James Madison, and Virginia governor Edmund Randolph—all held far less complacent views about the need for a more energetic Continental government than those serving in the governments of most of the states. Concluding their business on September 14, 1786, the twelve delegates endorsed an address prepared by Hamilton; that address asked "with the most respectful deference" that the states appoint commissioners to meet in Philadelphia in May of the coming year, "to devise such further provisions as should appear to them necessary to render the constitution of the Federal Government adequate to the exigencies of the Union." This seemed like a modest proposal, but underlying that request was a very ambitious agenda. The men in Annapolis were not interested in minor adjustments to the provisions of the Articles of Confederation; they were, in fact, hoping to launch a revolution in government.

Their plans for this revolution would first have to gain the approval of the Continental Congress in New York. The Congress received the address from the Annapolis Convention on September 20, and then ignored it for three weeks before finally referring it to a "grand committee" consisting of a delegate from each of the thirteen states. And there the proposal for a convention languished. Some of the inactivity stemmed from the reservations of a few committee members, who thought that the Congress had no right to call such a convention, but the more important reason for the Congress's inaction stemmed from its inability to get a sufficient number of delegates together to take up the matter at all. More than four more months would pass before, finally, on February 21, 1787, Congress took action. Some of the credit for that first positive step belongs to James Madison; in spite of bouts of illness, he made the trip from Virginia to New York to urge action on the Annapolis proposal. Perhaps more important, even though the Shaysite rebels in western Massachusetts had been dispersed by an imposing military force just two weeks before, the Continental Congress continued to receive news that the Commonwealth of Massachusetts was in a state of rebellion.

When the Continental Congress finally approved the proposal that a meeting of delegates from each of the states be held in Philadelphia in May, it did so with the understanding that the convention would meet "for the sole and express purpose of revising the Articles of Confederation, and reporting to Congress and the several legislatures such alterations and provisions therein as shall when agreed to in Congress and confirmed by the States, render the federal Constitution adequate to the exigencies of Government and the preservation of the Union." The congressional delegates, reluctantly agreeing to the idea of a convention, had done everything they could in their resolution of approval to limit the charge of that convention. But those constraints would soon be ignored by a handful of delegates to the Constitutional Convention who had a far more ambitious idea for a federal union in mind.

THE CONVENTION DELAYED

It did not begin auspiciously. On May 14, 1787, the day on which the Convention was due to begin, James Madison, who had arrived in Philadelphia eleven days before, found himself in a gloomy mood. Only a handful of delegates had turned up, and indeed eleven more days would pass before the Convention was finally able to get under way with a bare quorum of seven state delegations assembled. General Washington, one of the few who had arrived in Philadelphia on time, began to worry that the Constitutional Convention would fall victim to the same combination of apathy and indolence that had afflicted the Continental Congress. As things turned out, however, that eleven-day hiatus would provide for those few delegates who had bothered to turn up on time a rare opportunity to plan their revolution in government.

The ringleader was the thirty-seven-year-old Madison. Standing only a few inches over five feet tall, scrawny, suffering from a combination of poor physical health and hypochondria, and painfully awkward in any public forum, Madison nevertheless possessed a combination of intellect, energy, and political savvy that would mobilize the effort to create an entirely new form of continental union.

Madison was gradually joined, over the days between May 14 and May 25, by a group of delegates from Virginia and Pennsylvania who would combine to concoct a plan not merely to "amend" the Articles of Confederation, but to set the proceedings of the Convention on a far more ambitious course. The first gathering of these reform-minded delegates took place on the evening of May 16, in the home of Benjamin Franklin, where dinner was served in his impressive new dining room along with a "cask of Porter," which, Franklin reported, received "the most cordial and universal approbation" of all those assembled. The Pennsylvania and Virginia delegates would thereafter meet frequently during the days leading up to May 25, both in the afternoons in the state house itself and in the evenings in City Tavern or the Indian Queen, to craft an entirely new conception of Continental government.

Franklin's and Washington's presence gave the group

both dignity and prestige, but it was Madison and James Wilson and Gouverneur Morris of Pennsylvania who provided much of the intellectual leadership. Wilson, a dour but brilliant Scotsman, was perhaps the only person in the Convention who was Madison's intellectual equal, and he shared Madison's commitment to creating a truly "national" government based on the consent of the people, not the individual states. Gouverneur Morris was nearly as intellectually brilliant as Wilson; he shared with Wilson a desire for a strong national government, but his personality was very different—more mercurial and outgoing (particularly when it came to his amorous relationships with women). And he was also more openly contemptuous of the excesses of "democracy." Together these men would forge a radical new plan, the Virginia Plan, which would shape the course of events during that summer of 1787.

THE CONVENTION GOES TO WORK

By seizing the initiative, this small group of nationalist-minded politicians was able to set the terms of debate during the initial stages of the Convention, gearing the discussion toward not *whether*, but *how* a vastly strengthened Continental government would be constructed. On May 25, 1787, the Convention finally gathered the necessary number of delegates to open its business, and the following Monday, May 28, the delegates agreed to a proposal that would prove invaluable in allowing men like Madison, Wilson, and Morris to move their plan forward. To prevent the "licentious publication of their proceedings," the delegates agreed to observe a strict rule of secrecy, with "nothing spoken in the house to be printed or otherwise published or communicated." One consequence of this decision was that the delegates were forced to deliberate throughout that Philadelphia summer—with the average daytime temperature in July and August hovering in the eighties and nineties and the intense humidity for which the city is still famous—with the doors of the Assembly Room closed and its windows shut. The more important consequence, amazingly, at least in terms of twenty-first-century political practices, was that the delegates were scrupulous in adhering to the rule of secrecy. Barely a world of their deliberations leaked out of the Convention during the whole of the summer.

Virtually all the delegates took it for granted that the rule of secrecy was wholly appropriate; in the words of Virginia's George Mason, it was "a necessary precaution to prevent misrepresentations or mistakes; there being a material difference between the appearance of a subject in its first crude and undigested shape, and after it shall have been properly matured and arranged."

But was such secrecy appropriate to a democratic republic? Our answer today, of course, would be no. Yet the delegates, if they had had to answer the question, would have been quick to remind us that the political values they were serving, while definitely "republican," were not "democratic." As firm believers in republican values, they were committed to creating a political system that rejected any form of hereditary rule, and that was broadly representative of the public at large—but their commitment to republican values did not extend to an endorsement of the notion that all men were equally qualified or equally entitled to play an active part in the creation of a new government.

Protected from a hostile public reaction by the rule of secrecy, the delegates proceeded to debate the Virginia Plan, the essential features of which were:

1. The creation of a "national" legislature consisting of two branches, with membership in each branch to be apportioned according either to "Quotas of contribution" or the "number of free inhabitants." This body would have the power to "legislate in all cases to which the separate States are incompetent" and to "negative all laws passed by the several States."
2. The creation of a powerful "National Executive," to be elected by the national legislature.
3. The chief executive, together with "a convenient number of the National Judiciary," would compose a "Council of revision," which could veto laws passed by either the national legislature or the various state legislatures.

As the details of the Virginia Plan were revealed to those gathered in the Assembly Room, it became clear that the plan was not a mere revision of the Articles of Confederation but, rather, a bold new start on an entirely new kind of government. The word "national" rather than "federal" was used repeatedly to describe the various branches of the proposed government, and the powers of that government were consistently defined as superior to those of the states. The Virginia Plan also reflected some of the reservations that its authors had with respect to democratic political processes. Of all the branches of the government, only the lower house was to be directly elected by the people; officials in the other branches were to be either indirectly elected or appointed.

Some within the Convention were outraged by the audacity of the plan. James Madison, casting his eyes around the Assembly Room as Virginia governor Edmund Randolph delivered the speech outlining the details of the Virginia Plan, observed a variety of reactions: emphatic agreement among the Virginia and Pennsylvania delegates; mild approval from New York delegate Alexander Hamilton; but clear disapproval from the other two members of the New York delegation, Robert Yates and John Lansing.

Even more striking, New Jersey delegate William Paterson was clearly shocked by what he was hearing. A highly intelligent but rigid and puritanical soul, Paterson would emerge as one of the principal spokesmen for the interests of the smaller, less-populous states. Paterson could be seen frantically scribbling on a notepad: "Objection!" He, like Robert Yates, believed that the adoption of the Virginia Plan would create a "consolidated union in which the idea of the states should be nearly annihilated."

But Paterson and Yates, observing the rule of secrecy, confined their outrage to the Assembly Room of the state house. As it would turn out, the rule of secrecy operated powerfully in favor of those delegates who wished to see such drastic change. Had a strong advocate of the sovereign power of the individual states—such as Virginia's Patrick Henry, who was elected a delegate to the Convention but declined to serve—heard of this radical deviation from the instructions of the Continental Congress, he would have mounted his horse and rode to Philadelphia to join his delegation. But Henry and other politicians jealous of guarding the power of their states were not apprised of the proceedings, and for that reason, on May 30—just three days after the Convention began its work—a majority of state delegations, with six of the eight states present voting in favor, agreed that "a national government ought to be established consisting of a supreme Legislative, Executive, and Judiciary." They had voted for a revolution in the structure of America's Continental government.

It was an amazing victory for that small cadre of nationalist-minded delegates who had cooked up the Virginia Plan, but their attempt at revolutionary change, once launched, proved difficult both to sustain and to control. Over the course of the summer, the delegates would debate, disagree, and ultimately compromise on a host of issues. The most divisive of those issues—those involving the apportionment of representation in the national legislature, the powers and mode of election of the chief executive, and the place of the institution of slavery in the new Continental body politic—would change in fundamental and unexpected ways the shape of the document that would eventually emerge on September 17, 1787.

THE FOUNDING FATHERS AND FEDERALISM

The delegates haggled over how to apportion representation in the legislature off and on for the entire period between May 30 and July 16. Those from large, populous states such as Virginia and Pennsylvania argued that representation in both houses should be based on population, while those from smaller states such as New Jersey and Maryland argued for equal representation for each state. The so-called New Jersey Plan, presented by William Paterson in mid-June, called for a "federal" rather than a "national" government, and its essential feature—a single-house legislature in which each state was to have only one vote—seemed to be a reincarnation of the Articles of Confederation. In fact, the New Jersey delegates, along with most of the delegates from other small states, were less concerned about limiting the power of the new government than they were interested in gaining maximum power for their states within the newly strengthened government.

The protracted debate over these alternatives was an unedifying, even unattractive, affair. At one point, Gunning Bedford, a corpulent, blustery delegate from Delaware, confronted the principal supporters of the Virginia Plan from Virginia, Pennsylvania, and Massachusetts, thundering, "I do not, gentlemen, trust you." Bedford then threatened that if the small states did not get their way they might well, in pursuit of an alternative union, "find some foreign ally of more honor and good faith."

The compromise that eventually emerged from that debate, championed most energetically by the delegates from Connecticut, was an obvious one—so obvious that it was proposed off and on by several delegates almost from the beginning of the contentious six-week period between the end of May and the middle of July: representation in the lower house would be apportioned according to population, with each state receiving equal representation in the upper house. In the final vote on the Connecticut Compromise, occurring on July 16, five states supported the proposal with four opposing, including Virginia and Pennsylvania, and one state divided. James Madison in particular was disconsolate. He was convinced that the compromise would destroy the very character of the national government he hoped to create. Indeed, the next morning Madison and several other large-state delegates met to consider whether they should leave the Convention altogether. In fact, not only did they not leave the Convention, but they managed to turn defeat into victory. In an astonishing reversal of his "original intent," Madison, during the debate over ratification of the Constitution, would use his "defeat" in the controversy over representation to fashion an entirely new definition of federalism. In "Federalist No. 39" he defended the proposed new constitution against its critics by praising the different modes of representation in the House and Senate—with the House representing the people of the nation at large and the Senate representing the residual sovereignty of the states—as one of the features that made the new government part national and part federal. No one knew how that new definition of federalism would actually work in practice, and it would remain a source of contention for much of the nation's early history. In this, as in so many areas, the so-called original meaning of the Constitution was not at all self-evident—even to the framers of the Constitution themselves.

THE FOUNDING FATHERS AND THE PRESIDENCY

The debate among the delegates over the nature of the American presidency was more high toned and, if anything, even more protracted and confusing than that over representation in the Congress. At one extreme, nationalists like James Wilson and Gouverneur Morris argued forcefully for a strong, independent executive capable of giving "energy, dispatch, and responsibility" to the government. They urged their fellow delegates to give the president an absolute veto over congressional legislation. At the other end of the spectrum, Roger Sherman, a plainly dressed, plainspoken delegate from Connecticut who would prove to be one of the most sagacious members of the Convention, spoke for many delegates when he declared that the "Executive magistracy" was "nothing more than an institution for carrying the will of the Legislature into effect." This led Sherman to the conclusion that the president should be removable from office "at pleasure" any time a majority in the legislature disagreed with him on an important issue. (By that same logic, Sherman would have allowed the president to be impeached by a majority of Congress for just about any reason at all.)

Many—perhaps most—of the delegates thought that the executive should be elected by the national legislature; still others thought the executive should be elected by the state legislatures or even by the governors of the states. James Wilson was virtually the only delegate who came out unequivocally for direct election of the president by the people. He believed that it was only through some form of popular election that the executive branch could be given both energy and independence.

James Madison kept changing his mind. His initial version of the Virginia Plan called for election of the president by the national legislature. And although he has subsequently gained the reputation of being one of the foremost proponents of the doctrine of separation of powers, he muddled things in the Convention by proposing a merging of the executive and judicial powers in a "Council of revision" composed of both the executive and a "convenient number of the National Judiciary." Madison gradually came around to the idea that the executive and judicial functions should be separated, but he continued to argue for the selection of the president by Congress up until the final days of the Convention. After reading Madison's notes on the debates in the Convention—our primary resource for learning about what happened inside the Pennsylvania State House that summer—one gets the sense that his eventual acquiescence to the idea of an electoral college as the method of presidential election was marked as much by weariness as by enthusiasm.

James Wilson, realizing that his proposal for direct popular election of the president was gaining no favor, proposed a version of the electoral college in early June, but the delegates didn't like that proposal any more than they liked his proposal for direct popular election, voting it down overwhelmingly at that point. They voted against some version of the proposal on numerous occasions between early June and early September of 1787, only agreeing to the version contained in our modern Constitution (modified slightly by the Twelfth Amendment) grudgingly and out of a sense of desperation, as the least problematic of the alternatives before them.

It has often been observed that much of the framers' difficulty in deciding how to elect the president was the result of their misgivings about democracy—their fear that the people of the nation could not be trusted to make a wise choice for their chief executive. In truth, it was not so much that the Founding Fathers distrusted the inherent *intelligence* of the people but, rather, that they had a very clear and realistic understanding of the *provincialism* of the American people. They understood that America's vast landscape, the poor state of its communications, and the diversity of its cultural character and economic interests would make it extremely difficult for any single candidate to gain a majority of the popular vote. How could a voter in Georgia know the merits of a candidate in New York or vice versa? Thus they very quickly cast aside James Wilson's proposal for direct election of the president as unworkable.

The other obvious solution—election by members of a national Congress whose perspective was likely to be continental rather than provincial—was ultimately rejected because of the problems it created with respect to the doctrine of separation of powers: the president, it was feared, would be overly beholden to, and therefore dependent upon, the Congress for his election. The creation of an electoral college was a middle ground, and while many delegates feared that locally selected presidential electors would be subject to the same sort of provincial thinking as ordinary citizens, they reluctantly came to the conclusion that it was the best they could do while still preserving an adequate separation of power between the executive and legislative branches. It was a highly imperfect solution to a real problem, but in the context of the times, there may well have been no better alternative.

THE FOUNDING FATHERS
AND SLAVERY

The delegates' commitment to principles of equality as articulated in the Declaration of Independence was, even in the case of free adult males, a limited one. (For example, most of the delegates supported the imposition of property qualifications for voters in their individual states.) But nowhere were those limitations more obvious than during those instances when the subject of slavery intruded into their deliberations. By 1787 slavery in America was in a state of decline. It remained a significant part of the social and economic fabric in five of the states represented in the Convention, but only two states—South Carolina and Georgia—were inclined to argue for an expansion of America's "peculiar institution." Yet the delegates in Philadelphia failed to eradicate that great contradiction to the core values of liberty and equality on which America had declared its independence. Instead, they enshrined the institution of slavery within their new Constitution.

Although neither the word "slave" nor "slavery" is mentioned anywhere in the Constitution, contention over slavery pervaded the debates on the Constitution throughout the whole of the summer of 1787. It was, for example, impossible to discuss questions relating to the apportionment of representation without confronting the fact that the slave population of the South—whether conceived of as residents or property—would affect the calculations for representation. The delegates argued about the proper formula for representing slaves through much of the summer. The final resolution of that issue—a formula by which slaves would be counted as three-fifths of a person in apportioning both representation and taxation—was a purely mechanical and amoral calculation designed to produce harmony among conflicting interests within the Convention. As many disgruntled delegates pointed out, it had little basis either in logic or morality, but in the end, the need for a consensus on the issue, however fragile that consensus might be, outweighed all other considerations.

The debate over the future of the international slave trade was in many respects more depressing than that which culminated in the three-fifths compromise. Only the delegates from South Carolina and Georgia were determined to continue what most other delegates believed to be an iniquitous trade, yet their insistence that the trade continue for at least another twenty years carried the day. However troubled delegates from the other states may have been, their concern for harmony within the Convention was much stronger than their concern for the fate of those Africans whose lives and labor would be sacrificed by the continuation of the slave trade.

Finally, the delegates adopted without dissent a provision requiring that any "Person held to Service or Labour in one State . . . [and] escaping into another, . . . shall be delivered up on Claim of the Party to whom such Service or Labour may be due." By means of that tortured language, and without mentioning either the word "slaves" or "slavery," the delegates made a fugitive-slave clause an integral part of our federal compact. It was the one act of the Convention that not only signaled the delegates' grudging acceptance of slavery but also made the states that had moved either to abolish or gradually eliminate slavery in the aftermath of the Revolution actively complicit in their support of that institution.

THE QUESTION OF
A BILL OF RIGHTS

On September 12, just five days before the Convention was to adjourn, George Mason of Virginia rose and expressed his wish that the nearly completed draft of the Constitution be "prefaced with a Bill of Rights." It would, he said, "give great quiet to the people." Citing as examples the bills of rights in the individual state constitutions, Mason believed that the delegates to the Philadelphia Convention might prepare a bill of rights "in a few hours."

Mason had good reason to make such a suggestion. As the principal draftsman of the Virginia Declaration of Rights, he believed that bills of rights articulating the fundamental liberties of the citizenry should be part of any proper constitution. And as the delegates to the Convention would discover in the coming months, there were a good many in America—probably a majority of citizens—who shared that belief. But the delegates must have groaned audibly at Mason's suggestion. Roger Sherman of Connecticut quickly disagreed with Mason, arguing that since there was nothing in the proposed Constitution that was contrary to the provisions in the various state bills of rights, there was no need to duplicate them by adding a bill of rights to it. Mason fought back, insisting that a federal bill of rights guaranteeing that the new government would not encroach on the people's fundamental liberties—such as freedom of speech, press, and religion, and trial by jury—was essential if those liberties were to be protected. But the delegates turned a deaf ear. When the matter was put to a vote, after a discussion lasting no more than a few moments, not a single state delegation supported Mason's proposal.

That decision, arrived at hastily and casually, would prove to be one of the most serious mistakes made by the men who drafted the Constitution. When Thomas Jefferson, serving as ambassador to France, received a copy of the completed Constitution from James Madison, he was unable to contain his unhappiness at the absence of a bill of rights. "The omission of a bill of rights, providing clearly and without the aid of sophisms, for freedom of religion, freedom of the press, protection against standing armies, restriction against monopolies, the eternal and unremitting force of the habeas corpus laws, and trials by jury in all matters," was, Jefferson wrote in dismay to his friend, a grievous error. He believed that a bill of rights was an essential protection "against doing evil, which no government should decline," and he expressed the hope that a bill of rights would be added to the Constitution without delay.

How could the delegates have ignored the lessons of their revolutionary past and not included a bill of rights in their proposed plan of union? In the months following, as they tried to persuade a skeptical public to endorse the document, supporters of the Constitution would argue that the proposed federal government was primarily concerned "with objects of a general nature," and that any attempt to replicate the state bills of rights would be not only redundant but also dangerous. "Who will be bold enough," James Wilson asked, "to undertake to enumerate all the rights of the people?" His fear was that if the enumeration of those rights was not complete, then everything not explicitly mentioned would be presumed not to be a right at all. Madison was equally cavalier, calling the state bills of rights "parchment barriers" that had not served to stop the state governments from invading the rights of their citizens when it suited their purpose.

In fact, these glib rationalizations were probably not the real reasons for the omission of a bill of rights. By mid-

September the delegates were profoundly weary of their labors and desperately anxious to return to the comfort of their homes. Although Mason had claimed that "a bill might be prepared in a few hours," the delegates in the hot, stuffy Assembly Room knew better. It would be a difficult, arduous task filled with contention. And they wanted to go home. They would, however, pay a price for their impatience in the coming months.

"APPROACHING SO NEAR TO PERFECTION"

As the Convention prepared to adjourn, the delegates were hardly of one mind about the nature of the government they had created. Some, like Madison, had come with the intention of creating a truly supreme, "national" government, but by the end of the summer most delegates were referring to the proposed government as "federal" in its character. In fact, the framers—still fearful of the aggressive, corrosive effects of unrestrained power—tried to strike a balance between the two by creating a government of limited powers that nevertheless had the requisite "energy" to do all the things promised in the preamble: "to form a more perfect Union, establish Justice, insure domestic Tranquility, provide for the common defence, promote the general Welfare, and secure the Blessings of Liberty." A tall order, especially when they were pledging at the same time to create a government that divided power between the states and the nation in such a way as to allay people's fears of an overbearing central power. As the delegates made their decisions about whether to sign the Constitution on September 17, 1787, there was little common understanding among them about how this new part-national, part-federal conception of federalism would actually work in practice, but they had at least made a start in creating a framework within which issues of state and national power could be negotiated.

Similarly, most of the framers understood that it was necessary to invigorate executive power, but at the same time they wished to avoid at all costs creating anything that resembled the unchecked power of the British king. By rendering the selection of the president independent of the legislature and by giving that president a limited veto power over congressional legislation, the framers were on the whole remarkably successful in both invigorating and containing executive power. Successive generations have debated where the balance point between invigoration and containment should rest, but the framers were relatively successful in setting the general parameters for that debate.

The framers' greatest failure occurred in the area of slavery and race. It is perhaps unrealistic to expect these eighteenth-century men to have moved decisively against the institution of slavery, but they failed to seize the opportunity to take even minimal steps that might have eased the way toward the ultimate abolition of slavery. By creating a process by which the Constitution could be amended, they did provide for a way in which their initial mistakes could be corrected, but since the Constitution required the approval of three-quarters of the states for any amendment to take effect, those states that had a vested interest in keeping the institution of slavery in place had an effective veto power over anything that might substantially threaten it. It would take a bloody, ghastly civil war and the loss of six hundred thousand American lives to effect the kind of constitutional change that would eliminate the most fundamental paradox at the nation's core.

ON THAT FINAL DAY OF THE CONSTITUTIONAL Convention, it was left to the Convention's oldest delegate, eighty-one-year-old Benjamin Franklin, to sum up the nearly four months of debate, disagreement, and occasional outbursts of ill temper that had marked the proceedings of that summer. Franklin observed that whenever "you assemble a number of men to have the advantage of their joint wisdom, you inevitably assemble with those men all their prejudices, their passions, their errors of opinion, their local interests, and their selfish views. From such an assembly can a perfect production be expected?" The wonder of it all, Franklin asserted, was that the delegates had managed to create a system of government "approaching so near to perfection as it does."

Franklin acknowledged that there were "several parts of this Constitution which I do not at present approve," but, he added, "the older I grow the more apt I am to doubt my own judgment and pay more respect to the judgment of others." Franklin concluded by asking each of his fellow delegates to "doubt a little of his own infallibility" and step forward to sign the Constitution. In that spirit of humility, thirty-nine of the forty-two delegates present on that last day would take that important step forward and, in the process, move America one step forward in achieving a "more perfect Union."

CHAPTER FOUR

THE CONTEST OVER RATIFICATION

AMERICA'S FIRST NATIONAL REFERENDUM

As the delegates to the Philadelphia convention made their way back to their home states, the words engrossed on the four sheets of parchment they had drafted that summer represented little more than opinion. They lacked the sanction of the Continental Congress, the state governments, or "We the People." By the terms of the proposed Constitution, the new government would take effect when nine of the thirteen states, deliberating in specially called ratifying conventions, added their assent to the document. This was yet another of the revolutionary provisions of the proposed Constitution, as under the terms of the Articles of Confederation unanimous approval of all thirteen state legislatures was necessary for any amendment to take effect. But having already made the decision not to amend the Articles but, instead, to create an entirely new scheme of government, the framers devised a ratification procedure aimed at avoiding the necessity of unanimous approval.

The debate over the proposed Constitution in the individual states was America's first national referendum—the first time voters in all the states were asked to express their opinion about a specific subject. Unlike in state or local elections, where multiple candidates and multiple issues could often produce ambiguous results, the decision facing Americans during the ratification debates was a stark one: yes or no.

The debate over ratification was, first and foremost, a partisan political contest. In that contest supporters of the Constitution enjoyed some important advantages. In what would prove to be a brilliant tactical move, they appropriated the name Federalists from their opponents, leaving those who opposed ratification with the unappealing label of Anti-Federalists. In fact, most scholars agree that the true "federalists," in the original meaning of that word, were the opponents of the Constitution, who continued to believe in a central government of strictly limited powers, operating within the framework of a confederation of independent and sovereign states.

Equally important, the Federalists were able to capitalize on a key factor working in their favor: *momentum.* They immediately sent the proposed Constitution to the Continental Congress, and then persuaded the Congress to release the document to the states for their consideration within eleven days after the Convention adjourned. At that point supporters of the Constitution—many of whom had served in the Constitutional Convention and were already well prepared with arguments defending their actions—stole the initiative from their opponents. Many Anti-Federalists, though alarmed at the extent of the changes proposed by the Constitution, had not yet had time to formulate coherent arguments against ratification. Between the end of September and January 9, five states—Delaware, Pennsylvania, New Jersey, Georgia, and Connecticut—ratified the Constitution. Only in Pennsylvania was there significant opposition, and even in that state the superior organizational abilities of the Federalists—in particular, their control of most of the newspapers reporting on the debate over the Constitution—enabled them to prevail in the state ratifying convention by a two-to-one margin. As the Constitution was transmitted to the remaining states, the conventions in those states were confronted not only with a decision about whether or not to adopt the Constitution but also with the fact that more than half of the necessary nine states had already decided to do so.

Nevertheless, opponents of the Constitution in Massachusetts, the sixth state to consider the document, put up a fight. Massachusetts was the third-most-populous state in the union. It had been in the forefront of the fight to protect American liberty in the years leading up to independence, and at least of a few of its principal leaders—Samuel Adams and John Hancock in particular—had not participated in the Constitutional Convention and were known to be skeptical about the proposed Constitution. As the Massachusetts convention opened for business in mid-January, most observers calculated that the delegates were at best evenly divided and, possibly, leaning toward rejecting the Constitution.

As the debate on the Constitution unfolded, many of its critics focused on the absence of a bill of rights, and this issue became a rallying point for opposition in Massachusetts. The supporters of the Constitution, sensing that they might lose the battle for ratification, gave way, holding out the promise that they would add a bill of rights in the form of amendments as soon as government under the new Constitution commenced. Although many of the opponents of the Constitution demanded amendments as a *precondition* to ratification, the promise of subsequent amendments was sufficient to bring influential delegates such as John Hancock and Samuel Adams over to the side of the Federalists. By a slim margin—187 to 168—the Massachusetts convention ratified the Constitution on February 6, 1788.

The issue of prior versus subsequent amendments would be a part of the debate in all the remaining states considering the Constitution, but as the number of states agreeing to adopt the Constitution approached the necessary nine, momentum continued to favor the Federalists. Rhode Island, which had refused to attend the Convention in Philadelphia, declined even to call a ratifying convention in March of 1788, but following Rhode Island's rejection, Maryland agreed to the Constitution in April and South Carolina added its assent in May, bringing the total in the Federalist win column to eight. New Hampshire and Virginia debated the Constitution in June, and although New Hampshire's ratification on June 21, 1788, made adoption of the Constitution official, the debate in Virginia—the nation's most populous state and home to George Washington, the man who was everyone's choice to be president of the new United States—was considered by many to be crucial to the success or failure of the new union.

Virginia was also home to Patrick Henry, second only to Washington in popularity in his home state and perhaps the most formidable opponent of the Constitution in America. When George Washington sent him a copy of the Constitution soon after the Philadelphia Convention adjourned, Henry was nearly speechless with anger at the way in which the Convention had exceeded its authority. Responding to Washington's letter transmitting the copy of the Constitution to him, Henry maintained a polite and civil tone, but he was deeply unhappy, telling Washington that his distress over the document was "really greater than I am able to express." From that moment on, Henry worked tirelessly to prevent the adoption of the Constitution in his home state.

The battle in the Virginia ratifying convention featured Henry in the opposition against the Constitution's principal architect, James Madison. Henry, the firebrand of the Revolution in Virginia, scaled new oratorical heights in denouncing the Constitution's tendencies toward a "consolidated government." Madison calmly, systematically, and masterfully rebutted Henry's criticisms. In the end, the issue of prior versus subsequent amendments shaped the outcome. When the Virginia convention finally voted on the Constitution on June 25, 1788, the Federalists narrowly prevailed, eighty-nine to seventy-nine—but only after agreeing to propose to the First Federal Congress "whatsoever amendments may be deemed necessary."

At that point it became clear that a new government under a new constitution would go forward, but one of the young country's most populous and prosperous states, New York, had yet to consider the document. Two of the three New York delegates to the Constitutional Convention, John Lansing and Robert Yates, had staunchly opposed the Constitution every step of the way in Philadelphia. They continued their opposition during the ratification debate in New York, and, to make matters more difficult for supporters of the Constitution, New York's governor, George Clinton, was believed to dislike the proposed Constitution as well. It looked like the Constitution would go down to defeat in that state, but when news of Virginia's ratification reached New York, it became harder for the voters there to contemplate a life outside the strong union that was by then a foregone conclusion. As a consequence, New York ratified in late July of 1788, followed by the two laggards: North Carolina, in November of 1789, and Rhode Island, in May 1790.

The American people, with memories of the excesses of British rule still fresh in their minds, continued to be fearful of an overly centralized government, yet the Federalists had persuaded a substantial majority of those people to overcome their fears and adopt a Constitution giving the new federal government vastly increased powers. Some of their success in doing so was owed simply to their superior preparation and organizational skills; they had seized the initiative and swung a largely uniformed populace over to their side. But the ratification contests also produced an impressive body of political writing, some of it rising above its primary purpose of political persuasion to achieve enduring intellectual importance.

Between late September 1787 and the fall of 1788, several hundred pamphlets and newspaper essays appeared, both supporting and opposing ratification of the Constitution. The most influential of these were the eighty-five essays written by Alexander Hamilton, James Madison, and John Jay, which appeared under the pseudonym Publius. Hamilton, who had argued in the Constitutional Convention in Philadelphia for a government based closely on the aristocratic English constitution, had played an insignificant—perhaps even harmful—role in that body, but he was the man most responsible for orchestrating the writing of what came to be called *The Federalist Papers*. Although Hamilton was not wholly pleased with the final product of the Constitutional Convention's labors—he thought the proposed government was too weak and too "democratic"—he took the initiative to recruit James Madison and John Jay to join him in the effort. Although before the spring of 1788 they did not circulate much beyond New York, and therefore may not have had much of an impact on the ratification contest in most states, *The Federalist Papers* have by now achieved the status of a canonical text of American government and constitutionalism. Extended excerpts from three of the most important of those essays—numbers 10, 51, and 78—are included in this volume to give readers an appreciation for the extraordinarily high quality of political discourse in the founding era.

Although there was no single set of Anti-Federalist writings that matched *The Federalist* (as the first compilation of the papers was titled) either in its immediate impact or its influence on subsequent generations, Anti-Federalist writers did publish more than two hundred pamphlets and broadsides in opposition to the Constitution. Because Anti-Federalist critics raised every objection they could possibly devise in their attempt to defeat the Constitution, their critique lacks the intellectual coherence of *The Federalist*, but the broad themes of that critique—a distrust of concentrations of government power, and an emphasis on the role of ordinary citizens in preventing government encroachments on the people's liberty—have proven to be of enduring importance in American constitutional discourse.

As the debate over the Constitution concluded and the new government prepared to begin its operations, there remained fundamental differences of opinion among America's political leaders and the country's citizens about the meaning of the words crafted by the framers on the four parchment pages during that summer in 1787. The men who drafted the Constitution were not political philosophers but, rather, eighteenth-century politicians confronted with a daunting array of competing interests, provincial attachments, and real-life problems as they sought to hammer out a workable form of federal union. The form the eventual document would take was legal, but the process by which they arrived at the final language of the document was intensely political. After nearly four months of debate, disagreement, and numerous compromises (some of which, like those involving slavery, would come back to haunt the young nation), they finally arrived at a fragile consensus, producing a constitution that was, as Benjamin Franklin admitted, far from a "perfect production."

Whatever pride the framers may have taken in their achievement, few would have claimed that the language they had crafted was somehow immutable. They were all too aware that many of the compromises that had allowed them to reach their fragile consensus on September 17—most notably, those involving the division of power between state and federal governments within a new form of federal union, and the multiple compromises relating to the powers and mode of election of the executive branch—might serve to confuse, not clarify, the "ordinary meaning" of the words in the document they had devised. And once the new government under the Constitution commenced its operations, they would become even more acutely aware of the differences of constitutional opinion that would continue to divide them. The framers of the Constitution who met in Philadelphia in the summer of 1787 can be justly praised for creating a plan of government that was, in George Washington's words, "so little liable to well-founded objections." The popularly elected delegates to the state ratifying conventions helped give the people's sanction to that plan. But the work of creating an American nation, governed under the Constitution, still lay ahead.

CHAPTER FIVE

ESTABLISHING GOVERNMENT UNDER THE CONSTITUTION, 1789–1801

JAMES MADISON ONCE REMARKED THAT it was the thirteen state ratifying conventions that breathed "life and validity" into the Constitution; with the assent of those ratifying conventions, the constitutional history of America *as a nation* was about to begin. As historian Bernard Bailyn has written, the Constitution amounted to no more than "words on paper" until President George Washington and the First Federal Congress began to implement the theoretical principles enunciated in that document. From that time forward, America's constitutional history would be shaped by political leaders and ordinary citizens alike, as they sought to implement the new nation's experiment in union.

It is no accident that George Washington has gone down in history as "the Father of His Country." It is not merely that he had been commander in chief during the colonies' most perilous hour, in the American War for Independence, or that he reluctantly came out of retirement to serve as president of the Convention that brought the Constitution into being. His active presence may have been indispensable on each of those occasions, but his role as America's first president was of even greater importance. He knew that in spite of the words written on the parchment pages of the Constitution, the new federal government and the union it was intended to achieve were held together by tenuous threads. He knew that every action he took as the nation's first chief executive would be critically important in adding substance to the bare superstructure created by the Constitution, and that those actions would serve as precedent for subsequent generations.

President Washington took his oath of office in the Senate Chamber of Federal Hall in New York on April 30, 1789. The Constitution prescribes the precise words of the presidential oath: "I do solemnly swear (or affirm) that I will . . . to the best of my Ability, preserve, protect and defend the Constitution of the United States." As he took that first oath of office, Washington set a precedent that, down to the present day, most presidents would follow: he added to the end of the oath the phrase "so help me God," thereby injecting the deity into a government that was, by the terms of the Constitution itself, entirely separate from matters of religion or the church. His inaugural address—itself a precedent-setting event—was quintessential Washington: it combined an outward humility about his abilities to carry out the enormous responsibilities of the office with a dignified and self-confident manner that left no one in the audience with any doubt about his ability to shoulder those responsibilities.

As Washington was assuming the responsibilities of the presidency, the First Federal Congress, which had been in session since early March, was already hard at work fulfilling the most important promise made by the Federalists during the ratification debates: the promise that a bill of rights would be added to the Constitution. James Madison took the lead in steering a draft of a bill of rights through the Congress. On May 4, 1789, he announced his intention of introducing into the House of Representatives a set of amendments designed to "make the Constitution better in the opinion of those who are opposed to it." The content of what came to be known as the Bill of Rights was strongly influenced by similar bills of rights incorporated into the revolutionary state constitutions and, in particular, by the Virginia Declaration of Rights drafted by George Mason and adopted in June 1776. Congress approved a revised set of twelve amendments on September 25, and sent them to the states for ratification. Two of the amendments—one dealing with the apportionment of representation in the House of Representatives and the other prohibiting Congress from granting pay raises to its members before another election had been held—were not ratified by the states, but by December 15, 1791, the necessary number of states had ratified the other ten, and the Bill of Rights became a part of the United States Constitution.

The president's cabinet, consisting of the most senior officers of the executive branch below the president himself, is only hinted at in the Constitution. Article II, Section 2, gives the president the power to appoint, with the consent of a majority of the members of the Senate, "Ambassadors, other public Ministers and Consuls, Judges of the supreme Court, and all other Officers of the United States, whose Appointments are not herein otherwise provided for." But the Constitution is silent on how the "other Officers" of the executive branch are to be appointed. In the absence of specific wording on the subject, the First Congress took the lead in creating a system of administrative departments that would work with the president in carrying out the duties of the executive branch. The Congress began steps to create three departments during its first months of operation: the Department of Foreign Affairs (which in revised form became the Department of State), whose first secretary would be Thomas Jefferson; the Department of the Treasury, headed up by Washington's brilliant and loyal Revolutionary War aide-de-camp, Alexander Hamilton; and the Department of War, whose first secretary was another military compatriot of Washington's, General Henry Knox.

The debate over the creation of the Department of Foreign Affairs led to some disagreement over whether Congress or the president had the power to remove a cabinet officer; the decision arrived at on that occasion was that the power belonged to the president. In fact, the matter remained a subject of contention between Congress and the president for more than a century, although the sole authority of the president to remove cabinet officials seems now very well established.

Congress was even more aggressive about asserting a role that was equal to that of the executive branch with respect to the Department of the Treasury. Since the power over the purse was considered to be the most important that Congress possessed, the members of the First Congress, in creating the office of secretary of the treasury, required that the secretary "give information to either branch of the legislature, in person or in writing . . . respecting all matters referred to him." Although the secretary of the treasury has proven to be primarily an agent of executive power, Congress has always wished to keep close watch over the Treasury Department's activities.

Congress's other significant action during its first session was to fill in some of the Constitution's missing pieces with respect to the federal judiciary. The sections in the Constitution on the structure and powers of the judiciary are exceptionally vague. Article III states simply that "the judicial power of the United States shall be vested in one supreme Court, and in such inferior Courts as the Congress may from time to time ordain and establish." The courts' powers were similarly vague: they would have authority in "all Cases, in Law and Equity, arising under this Constitution, the Laws of the United States, and Treaties made," but where that authority began and ended was anyone's guess. Almost immediately after the First Congress convened, a special judiciary committee, chaired by Connecticut's Oliver Ellsworth, a member of the Constitutional Convention in 1787 and a future chief justice of the Supreme Court, began meeting. In September 1789, Congress passed the Judiciary Act of 1789. It created a federal court structure that has remained largely unchanged up to the present day, with three levels of federal courts: in the bottom tier, a set of district trial courts that empanel juries and hear cases; circuit courts that hear serious crimes involving sums of money over five hundred dollars, as well as hearing appeals from the district courts; and finally, the Supreme Court, which stands at the top of the hierarchy and in certain instances hears cases brought to it from the circuit courts of appeals.

The Judiciary Act of 1789 stipulated that the Supreme Court would consist of six justices, a number expanded by Congress to seven in 1807, then to nine in 1837 (Congress expanded the number to ten in 1863, but in 1869 it was reduced once again to nine, where it has remained up to the present day). The act defined the authority of the court narrowly, although it did grant the Supreme Court jurisdiction over appeals from state courts on matters touching on federal law. Over time the Supreme Court has asserted its power to hear appeals from state courts more aggressively, but in 1789 the precise jurisdiction of the Supreme Court with respect to state court cases was anything but clear. Initially, judges of the circuit courts were drawn from both the district courts and the Supreme Court, with the result being that Supreme Court justices had the arduous duty not only of doing their designated jobs but also of riding circuit in various regions of the country hearing cases on appeal from the district courts. Although the Judiciary Act of 1789 went part of the way toward putting flesh on the bare-bones structure of the federal judiciary as defined in the Constitution, the development of the judicial branch as a powerful component of the triad of executive, legislative, and judicial power remained unrealized in 1789.

Finally, the Judiciary Act of 1789 took one other important step in helping to shape the president's cabinet by creating the office of attorney general, a position that President Washington immediately filled with the appointment of his friend and former Virginia governor Edmund Randolph.

The question of whether and under what circumstances the president should exercise a veto over congressional legislation was a subject of considerable disagreement in the Constitutional Convention. The final language of Article I, Section 7, stipulates that the president can veto a law passed by Congress, but Congress retains the right to override the veto if two-thirds of the members of both houses choose to do so. In 1792 Washington received a bill from Congress that would have given some districts more than the one member of the House of Representatives for every thirty thousand inhabitants spelled out in the Constitution. Accordingly, Washington vetoed the bill on the grounds that it was in violation of the language of the Constitution. His veto did not provoke significant opposition in the Congress, but it would be his only veto of a congressional bill. Indeed, neither of his immediate successors, John Adams and Thomas Jefferson, would make use of the veto power, and it would not be until the presidency of Andrew Jackson that a chief executive would veto a bill, not on constitutional grounds, but rather because he disagreed with the policies proposed by the bill.

President Washington was the most influential in setting constitutional precedents that would determine the way the government would operate in subsequent generations, but the policies proposed by his secretary of the treasury, Alexander Hamilton, would play a hugely important role in enhancing the powers of the new federal government and, in the process, precipitate the first important constitutional debate in the young nation's history.

During the years 1790–91, Hamilton put forward ambitious proposals to put the young nation's finances and economy on a stronger footing. Hamilton proposed not only to pay off the debts incurred by the Continental government during the Revolutionary War but also to assume responsibility for the debts of the individual state governments. He hoped to establish the precedent that the federal government, and not the state governments, was the entity responsible for overseeing the financial well-being of the nation's economy. There was heated opposition to Hamilton's plan from those who feared that his proposal to pay off the state debts amounted to usurpation of state power, but Hamilton's proposals passed Congress and were signed into law by President Washington. Next, Hamilton proposed the creation of a national bank: the Bank of the United States. In one sense Hamilton's proposed bank was to operate like a private corporation, with a board of directors composed largely of private citizens and with a responsibility to return a profit to its shareholders. But it was also intended to function as a public entity, with the authority to handle many of the government's financial policies and transactions.

Congress passed the bank bill in February 1791 and transmitted it to President Washington for his approval. Mindful that many in Congress had strong objections to yet another Hamiltonian attempt to centralize power in the hands of the federal government, Washington sought opinions on the bill's constitutionality from both Hamilton and the secretary of state, Thomas Jefferson. Jefferson objected to the bill on two grounds. First, he argued that nowhere in the Constitution was the Congress empowered to charter a bank and that the Tenth Amendment, which reserves all powers not specifically enumerated in the Constitution to the states, rendered the bank bill unconstitutional. Jefferson then laid down the doctrine of what would come to be called "strict construction," arguing that the final paragraph of Article I, Section 8, of the Constitution, giving Congress the power to pass laws "necessary and proper" for carrying into effect the enumerated powers, needed to be interpreted narrowly. In Jefferson's reading of that clause, the so-called unenumerated powers of Congress needed to be "indispensable" or of an "invincible necessity." He could see no such necessity in Hamilton's bank bill. Hamilton, arguing for a broad construction of the "necessary and proper" clause, defined the clause as sanctioning actions by Congress that would be "useful," "needful," or "conducive" and defended his bill. President Washington, after considering the two arguments, sided with Hamilton and signed the bill into law, but the constitutional line of division between "strict constructionists" and "broad constructionists" would remain an important part of the debate on how to interpret the Constitution from that time right up to the present day.

The constitutional division articulated during the debate over the Bank of the United States, along with important differences of opinion over the proper conduct of American foreign policy, led to an entirely unexpected development in American life: the development of organized political parties. These divisions were initially only loosely formed coalitions in the United States Congress, but they were gradually transformed into self-conscious entities founded on a large popular base throughout the country as a whole. These nascent political parties began to appear during the second term of President Washington's administration, and then increased in importance and intensity during the administration of Washington's successor, John Adams. Those favoring a strict construction of the Constitution also tended to be wary of the Washington and Adams administrations' foreign policies. They believed those policies to be overly friendly to the monarchical government of Great Britain and insufficiently supportive of America's revolutionary ally France, which in 1789 had undergone its own revolution inspired in part by the principles of the American Revolution. James Madison, one of the architects of the Constitution and one of the leading Federalists supporting it during the ratification debates, joined with Thomas Jefferson as a leader of what would come to be called the Jeffersonian Republican Party. Although Alexander Hamilton was responsible for many of the policies that would define the agenda of what came to be known as the Federalist Party, President Washington and President Adams were chiefly responsible for implementing those policies.

As candidates for public office at all levels found it necessary to take positions on the issues that divided Federalists and Republicans, popular awareness of national political issues increased. More and more frequently, the outcome of elections, particularly to Congress, turned not on traditional notions of who might be the wisest or most virtuous candidate but, rather, on the party identification of the candidates. With the retirement of President Washington in 1796 (his decision not to seek a third term would constitute yet another unofficial constitutional precedent, one that held sway until 1940, when President Franklin D. Roosevelt successfully sought a third term), partisan attention began to focus on the election of the president.

Beginning in 1796, but reaching a higher level of sophistication in 1800, leaders of the two parties aggressively recruited voters to cast their ballots for presidential electors pledged in advance to the respective standard-bearers of the two parties. This would have a profound effect on the way in which one provision of Article II, Section 1, pertaining to the way the electoral college was to select a president, worked. The Constitution stipulates that the individual states will determine the manner in which electors are selected. In the beginning, some were elected from individual electoral districts, some were selected by a statewide ballot, and still others were selected by the state legislatures. But whatever the mode of selection, the framers of the Constitution assumed that those voting for the presidential and vice-presidential electors would do so on the basis of the prospective elector's standing in his state or local community, and that those elected to the position would then use their own independent judgment in casting their ballots in the electoral college. With the advent of political parties, candidates for elector now ran on the basis of their support for the presidential and vice-presidential nominees of the respective parties. In that fashion, the selection of the president and vice president, initially conceived as a process in which the people would be only indirectly involved, began to operate in a far more democratic fashion, with the two parties actively recruiting the voters to support their slates of electors.

In 1798, as the contest between the Republican and Federalist parties for control of the new government intensified during the administration of John Adams, the Federalist majority in Congress passed—and President Adams signed into law—the Alien and Sedition Acts, a set of acts aimed not only at seeking out and deporting dangerous aliens (who in the eyes of the Federalists were usually French), but also at punishing with fines and even imprisonment anyone who published or printed "false, scandalous, and malicious writing" against the government of the United States. In passing the law, the Federalists were defining their Republican opponents not as a "loyal opposition" but, rather, as enemies to the government. In an age where changes in government had traditionally come about only through illegal coups d'état or, as in the American case, by revolution, the Federalists, as the party in power, were simply not able to distinguish between honest differences of opinion over policy and treasonous behavior. Accordingly, they used the Alien and Sedition Acts to initiate criminal prosecutions against their political rivals.

The Alien and Sedition Acts, far from silencing the Republican opposition, only served to inflame it, with Republican pamphleteers and newspaper contributors becoming ever more vitriolic in their attacks on the Federalists, and the Federalists, in turn, becoming even more determined in their prosecution of their political opponents. This partisan warfare triggered the first constitutional crisis in the nation's young history. The Virginia legislature, acting under the leadership of James Madison, and the Kentucky legislature, spurred on by Thomas Jefferson, passed sets of resolutions declaring the Alien and Sedition Acts unconstitutional, as violations not only of the First Amendment guarantees of free speech and freedom of the press but also of the guarantees of the Tenth Amendment, which, Jefferson argued in his draft of the Kentucky Resolutions, reserved to the states power "over the freedom of religion, freedom of speech, [and] freedom of the press." What was truly novel about the Virginia and Kentucky Resolutions was their proposed remedy for this clash of constitutional interpretation between the states of Kentucky and Virginia, on the one hand, and the federal Congress on the other. The Virginia and Kentucky Resolutions asserted that since the federal Constitution was a compact among the individual states, it was the states themselves that had ultimate authority to determine the constitutionality of a federal law and, in the case of a federal law that threatened to interfere with the liberties of the people of the states, to "interpose" themselves as a means of "arresting the progress of evil." Jefferson's Kentucky Resolutions went even further, stating that since that state had found the Alien and Sedition Acts to be in violation of the U.S. Constitution, it had the right to declare the laws "altogether void and of no force." In a final, provocative statement, the Kentucky Resolutions averred that if the federal government continued to exercise its power oppressively, those actions might "drive these States into revolution and blood."

The Virginia and Kentucky Resolutions had ominous implications for the new union. By the reasoning of the resolutions, the individual states, not the Supreme Court of the United States, were the ultimate arbiters of the constitutionality of a federal law. Some thirty years later, John C. Calhoun of South Carolina would follow the logic of the Kentucky Resolutions in enunciating the doctrine of "nullification," the right of a state to render "null and void" any statute that was in that state's judgment unconstitutional. And by Calhoun's logic—and later that of Confederate president Jefferson Davis—the ultimate recourse of the states, as original parties to the federal compact, was that of secession from the union itself. At the time that Jefferson and Madison wrote the Virginia and Kentucky Resolutions, the concept of "judicial review," giving to the Supreme Court ultimate authority on issues relating to the interpretation of the Constitution, had not been fully established or accepted, although certainly many of the framers of the Constitution assumed that the Supreme Court might exercise such a function. That constitutional development lay in the future and would occur only after the constitutional crisis over the Alien and Sedition Acts was settled, not by courts or by force of arms but, rather, at the ballot box.

By the time of the presidential election of 1800, the Federalist and Republican parties had put into place more fully developed structures by which to recruit voters to their respective sides, and those advances in party organization, together with the overheated, partisan atmosphere created by disagreements over foreign policy and the Alien and Sedition Acts, made it one of the most vituperative and bitterly contested presidential elections in American history. The Federalists selected a slate consisting of the sitting president, John Adams, as their presidential candidate and Charles Cotesworth Pinckney of South Carolina as the vice-presidential candidate. The Republican ticket featured Thomas Jefferson as the presidential candidate and Aaron Burr of New York as the vice-presidential candidate. When the presidential electors had cast their ballots, the Republican slate received a majority of electoral votes, but party discipline among the Republican electors was so great that each of the electors cast each of their two ballots for Jefferson *and* Burr. Article II, Section 1, of the Constitution stipulates that each elector casts two ballots, and that the individual receiving the largest number of votes will be president and the individual receiving the second-highest number of votes will be vice president, but it does not differentiate between a presidential vote and a vice-presidential vote. Since Jefferson and Burr had received an equal number of electoral votes, there was no constitutional means by which to determine who was meant to be president and who vice president. So, again by the terms of Article II, Section 1, the election was thrown into the House of Representatives, where the state delegations in the House, with each state being given equal weight in the voting, would decide the outcome of the election. After a good deal of tumult and intrigue, in which the Federalists in the House seemed to be maneuvering to elect Burr rather than Jefferson (a scheme to which Burr did not seem to object!), the House, on the thirty-sixth ballot, finally elected Thomas Jefferson as the third president of the United States. But the whole affair demonstrated that the electoral college provision of the Constitution, as it was then constructed, was not well suited to an election process in which political parties were working diligently to organize the electorate behind both their presidential and vice-presidential candidates. The passage of the Twelfth Amendment in 1804, which stipulates that presidential and vice-presidential electoral ballots be separate and distinct, signaled a recognition of how the advent of political parties had changed the way the electoral college functioned, transforming it from an elitist institution into a democratic one. Of all of the events of the first twelve years of the new government's operation, the emergence of political parties—a development unanticipated and unwanted by the Founding Fathers and operating wholly outside the formal political and constitutional structures of the new federal union—would be paramount in transforming the American republic into a democratic republic.

CHAPTER SIX

SUPREME COURT DECISIONS THAT HAVE SHAPED AMERICA'S CONSTITUTIONAL HISTORY

THE STORY OF THE EVOLUTION OF THE United States Constitution continues even today. During the two and a quarter centuries since the Constitution took effect, the operations of the federal, state, and local governments have undergone remarkable changes. With those changes, successive generations of Americans have found that their relationship with those governments has also changed. The framers of the Constitution provided one explicit mechanism by which to alter the way the federal government does its business: as spelled out in Article V, Congress or, upon application of two-thirds of the state legislature, a specially called convention, may propose constitutional amendments. Those proposed amendments must then be approved by three-quarters of the state legislatures or state conventions before being adopted. The framers did not believe that amending the Constitution should be a quick or easy task, nor has it proven to be such. Only twenty-seven amendments have been enacted since the Constitution was first adopted, and ten of those—the Bill of Rights—were added only two years after the new government was launched.

But amendments have not been the only mechanism for constitutional change. All three branches of the federal government—the Congress, the executive, and the federal judiciary—have themselves been agents of change. An important part of the job of America's political leaders—elected and appointed—has been to respond to the extraordinary pace of social, economic, political, and cultural change that has marked the history of America since its first settlements. In responding to those changes, our political leaders have made decisions that have sometimes altered our understanding of the way the United States Constitution functions in serving "We the People."

This final chapter is not intended to describe all the events that have shaped the U.S. Constitution. Instead, it offers brief summaries of a select number of Supreme Court decisions that have had a profound influence on our constitutional history. The selection of decisions, from among the several thousand rendered by the Supreme Court since the federal government commenced operation in 1789, is admittedly a subjective one. There are no doubt many decisions that constitutional scholars might prefer to some that I have chosen to summarize here. But my choices are not arbitrary; they have been informed by four important recurring issues and themes in American history:

1. The gradual acceptance of the principle of equality as a central value in American life.
2. The ever-changing debate within America over the meaning of federalism—the relationship between our national, state, and local governments.
3. The continuing debate within America over the appropriate division of power among the three branches of our federal government: the Congress, the president, and the judiciary.
4. The steady expansion of the application and interpretation of the rights granted to all American citizens by the federal Bill of Rights and by subsequent amendments to the Constitution.

• • •

MARBURY V. MADISON (1803). ALTHOUGH MANY OF THE framers of the Constitution believed that the newly created Supreme Court might have the power to review the constitutionality of a federal law, the court's power of "judicial review" is not explicitly spelled out in the Constitution. In March 1801, just before his term of office expired, Federalist president John Adams made a series of "midnight appointments" of federal judges in a last-minute attempt to ensure that the federal judiciary would be staffed with judges loyal to his political principles. Most of those appointed to the judgeships were subsequently installed in their new positions, but several of them, including William Marbury, who had been appointed justice of the peace in the District of Columbia, did not have their commissions delivered to them before Adams left office. When Thomas Jefferson, a member of the opposing Republican Party, assumed the presidency, he refused to issue Marbury his judicial commission. Marbury then petitioned the Supreme Court, whose chief justice was now Jefferson's bitter political enemy John Marshall, asking the court to issue a writ of mandamus (an edict commanding a government official to perform a particular action) ordering James Madison, the secretary of state, to deliver his commission to him. Justice Marshall conceded to President Jefferson a small victory by refusing to order Madison to deliver Marbury's commission, but much more was at stake in the ruling than poor Marbury's position as justice of the peace.

Although Marshall believed that Marbury had a legitimate right to his commission, he went on to conclude that the Supreme Court had no legal authority to force Secretary of State Madison to issue the commission to him. Although a portion of the Judiciary Act of 1789 had given the Court the right to issue writs of mandamus, Marshall and his fellow justices ruled that that portion of the act was "repugnant to the Constitution." And then he made a bold leap, pronouncing:

> It is emphatically the province and duty of the Judicial Department to say what the law is. . . . So, if a law be in opposition to the Constitution, if both the law and the Constitution apply to a particular case, so that the Court must either decide that case conformably to the law, disregarding the Constitution, or conformably to the Constitution, disregarding the law, the Court must determine which of these conflicting rules governs the case. This is of the very essence of judicial duty. If, then, the Courts are to regard the Constitution, and the Constitution is superior to any ordinary act of the Legislature, the Constitution, and not such ordinary act, must govern the case to which they both apply.

With that statement, the Supreme Court held the Judiciary Act of 1789 to be unconstitutional and, in the process, asserted the power of judicial review—the right of the Supreme Court to strike down an act it believes to be unconstitutional. In asserting that right, the Supreme Court set the judicial branch, which had been viewed by the framers of the Constitution as the least powerful and least consequential of the three branches of government, on a course to becoming a genuinely coequal branch of government.

The decision in *Marbury v. Madison* was carefully crafted so as not to appear to assert a sweeping power of judicial review over all pieces of congressional or state legislation, and because the specific issue involved was a relatively narrow one, Marshall's ruling provoked little opposition. Indeed, the Supreme Court in subsequent years would only sparingly use its newly claimed power of judicial review over laws passed by Congress. It would not strike down another federal law until its ruling in the *Dred Scott* decision in 1857.

• • •

McCulloch v. Maryland (1819). As we have seen in chapter 5, the proposal by Secretary of the Treasury Alexander Hamilton to create a Bank of the United States, subsequently enacted by Congress and signed into law by President Washington, provoked two competing constitutional doctrines: the "strict constructionist" doctrine articulated by Thomas Jefferson and the "broad constructionist" doctrine favored by Hamilton.

In 1816 Congress reaffirmed the broad-constructionist principles underlying the creation of the First Bank of the United States by offering a new charter to a Second Bank of the United States. The state of Maryland attempted to challenge the constitutionality of the bank by imposing a tax on its Baltimore branch that would have effectively made it impossible for it to do its business. The Supreme Court, with John Marshall writing the decision, ruled that Maryland did not have the right to interfere with the bank's operations and, more important, also affirmed the constitutionality of the bank by using a broad-constructionist reasoning that there were "implied powers" in addition to those explicitly enumerated in Article II of the Constitution.

The *McCulloch* case was just one of many cases in which rulings of the Marshall court served to promote the nation's economic development while at the same time fashioning a new conception of federalism by strengthening the power of the federal government at the expense of the state governments. Among the most important of these cases are *Fletcher v. Peck* (1810), *Dartmouth College v. Woodward* (1819), and *Gibbons v. Ogden* (1824).

Dred Scott v. Sandford (1857). The framers of the Constitution in Philadelphia had conspicuously failed to deal with what historian Bernard DeVoto called the "paradox at the nation's core": the existence of the institution of chattel slavery in a nation founded on principles of liberty and equality. The consequences of that failure became all the more acute in the aftermath of America's war with Mexico (1846–48). At the conclusion of that war, the ambitiously expanding nation found itself with vast quantities of new territory acquired from the vanquished Mexican government. The question facing the U.S. government was, what would be the status of slavery in these newly acquired territories? This was an issue that had divided North and South since 1819, when Missouri, a slaveholding territory, had applied for admission to the union. Although the United States Congress had fashioned some temporary compromises between the interests of North and South (the Missouri Compromise of 1820, the Compromise of 1850, and the Kansas-Nebraska Act of 1854), it was becoming increasingly clear that the issue of the status of slavery in the territories had put the two sections of the country on a collision course.

The Supreme Court's ruling in the *Dred Scott* case may well be the worst decision in the history of the Court. It was a bad decision not merely because of its dubious constitutional logic (although there was some of that) but, more importantly, because it was rendered on the assumption that nine unelected judges could resolve an issue—that of slavery in the territories—that democratic majorities in the United States Congress had found themselves unable to resolve and that deeply divided the people of the country as a whole. Seven of the nine justices (five southern and two northern) ruled against the petition of Dred Scott, a Missouri slave who had been taken by his owner first into the free state of Illinois and then later into the free territory (under the terms of the Missouri Compromise) of Wisconsin. Scott claimed, therefore, that he should be considered a free man.

The justices ruled that because Scott was legally a form of property, he had no right to sue in a federal court and therefore was not entitled to his freedom. That could have been the end of the case, and although it would have denied Scott the freedom he sought, it would not have shaken the very foundations of the American union. But the justices did not stop there. Abandoning long-held traditions of "judicial restraint" (the principle that justices should generally defer to the legislative branch in their rulings and that they should as much as possible base their decisions on existing legal precedents), the justices in the majority in the *Dred Scott* decision went on to rule that the part of the Missouri Compromise prohibiting slavery north of the 36°30' latitude line violated Fifth Amendment protections of the ownership of property. By its expansive definition of the right to own slave property, the *Dred Scott* decision opened up the possibility that the right to own slaves could not be constitutionally prohibited in any territory of the United States. Any decision by the Supreme Court on an issue as explosive as that involving slavery in the territories would have been a controversial one, but the court, by abandoning principles of judicial restraint, made an already difficult situation even more so. The decision was hailed as a great victory by southern proslavery advocates, but it also served to heighten the sectional conflict between North and South and accelerated the course of the nation toward civil war.

PLESSY V. FERGUSON (1896). THE AMERICAN CIVIL WAR remains the most traumatic event in the nation's history. It was the result at least in part of the failure of the Constitution to provide a workable mechanism for resolving the increasingly bitter divisions between North and South over the issue of slavery. But one consequence of that bloody war, in which nearly six hundred thousand Americans lost their lives, was the opportunity to eliminate that paradox at the nation's core—the opportunity not only to abolish slavery but also to insert into the Constitution fundamental protections for the rights of freed slaves. The passage of the Thirteenth, Fourteenth, and Fifteenth Amendments was an important step in transforming the egalitarian rhetoric of the preamble of the Declaration of Independence into binding constitutional law. The language of the Fourteenth Amendment in particular, with its stipulation that no state can deprive "any person of life, liberty, or property, without due process of law" and its guarantee of "equal protection of the laws" to all citizens, seemed to offer the promise of an America whose Constitution and laws would finally be in harmony with the egalitarian rhetoric that had justified the revolt against British rule.

But those amendments were not in themselves sufficient to protect the rights of freemen, and in the face of continuing intransigence in the South, a northern, Republican-controlled Congress embarked on an attempt to "reconstruct" the states of the former Confederacy and, in the process, to ensure that the civil rights of newly freed slaves were not violated. The so-called era of Reconstruction had run its course by the mid-1870s, and as the commitment of white Americans to equal rights for all waned, many of the post–Civil War statutes aimed at ensuring equal protection under the law came under attack. The ruling in *Plessy v. Ferguson* was the culmination of that unfortunate trend.

During that same period, Congress and the courts were confronted with additional challenges with respect to civil rights. With the readmission of all the states of the former Confederacy, the guarantees of equal rights to freed slaves provided by the Fourteenth and Fifteenth Amendments were gradually weakened. Perhaps reflecting some fatigue from the political and sectional battles of the Reconstruction era, the rulings of the Supreme Court during the last three decades of the nineteenth century tended to weaken America's commitment to the Fourteenth Amendment's promise of equal protection under the law.

In the *Slaughter-House Cases* (1873), *United States v. Cruikshank* (1876), the *Civil Rights Cases* (1883), and finally in *Plessy v. Ferguson* (1896), the court steadily narrowed the extent to which the provisions of the Fourteenth Amendment could be used to prevent state governments or private companies and institutions from infringing on the rights of American citizens.

The decision in *Plessy* turned on the constitutionality of an 1890 Louisiana statute requiring separate railway cars for black passengers and white passengers. In 1892 Homer Plessy, a light-skinned African American working in concert with a group of African American professionals in New Orleans who wished to test the constitutionality of the law, boarded a "whites only" car and was promptly arrested. After the case had worked its way through the lower federal courts, which consistently ruled against Plessy, the Supreme Court agreed to hear the case in 1896.

In a seven-to-one decision, with one justice not participating, the Court rejected Plessy's contention that enforcing separation of the races in the railway cars was a violation of the "equal protection" clause of the Fourteenth Amendment. Justice Henry Billings Brown, who wrote the majority opinion, maintained that the "enforced separation of the two races" did not necessarily "stamp the colored race with a badge of inferiority." Then, revealing the full extent of the racial assumptions underlying the decision, he wrote:

> Legislation is powerless to eradicate racial instincts or to abolish distinctions based on physical differences, and the attempt to do so can only result in accentuating the difficul-

ties of the present situation. If the civil and political rights of both races be equal, one cannot be inferior to the other civilly or politically. If one race be inferior to the other socially, the Constitution of the United States cannot put them on the same plane.

Justice John Marshall Harlan, the only justice to side with Plessy, wrote an impassioned dissent. He scornfully rejected the argument supporting "separate but equal" facilities for the two races, and then asserted that "in view of the Constitution, in the eye of the law, there is in this country no superior, dominant, ruling class of citizens. There is no caste here. Our Constitution is color-blind, and neither knows nor tolerates classes among citizens. In respect of civil rights, all citizens are equal before the law."

Harlan's powerful dissent notwithstanding, the decision in *Plessy* would put into place the doctrine of "separate but equal," one that would serve to justify both state-sponsored and privately imposed segregation across a wide range of areas, from restaurants to public accommodations to public schools.

SCHENCK V. UNITED STATES (1919) AND GITLOW V. NEW YORK (1925). These two cases each deal with the free speech guarantees of the First Amendment, but the Gitlow case raised an additional question that has had important ramifications for constitutional interpretation up to the present day.

During the presidential administration of Woodrow Wilson, in the aftermath of World War I, the Supreme Court made one of its most important rulings dealing with issues of national security and free speech. In *Schenck v. United States*, the court upheld the Espionage Act of 1917, a congressional statute aimed at punishing anyone engaged in actions that might "be used to the injury" of the United States war effort. In that case, the Court ruled that the actions of Charles Schenck, a member of the Socialist Party who had distributed pamphlets opposing the draft during World War I, had produced such injury and therefore were not protected by the free speech guarantees of the First Amendment. In that decision Justice Oliver Wendell Holmes, Jr., noted that the right of free speech is not an absolute one, using the following example: "Free speech would not protect a man in falsely shouting fire in a theatre, and causing a panic." Holmes then offered a means of resolving the potential conflict between First Amendment guarantees of free speech and the need for public order: the question to be determined, Holmes reasoned, was whether the actions or words being employed "might create a clear and present danger" to cause "substantive evils." In general, the courts have tended to interpret the meaning of "clear and present danger" in a way that gives government greater powers to restrict free speech during times of war.

The case of *Gitlow v. New York* involved yet another Socialist, Benjamin Gitlow, accused of distributing subversive literature, and as in the *Schenck* case, the court upheld Gitlow's conviction. Indeed, the court modified the "clear and present danger" doctrine laid down by Justice Holmes and substituted a much looser standard—that of "dangerous tendency."

Perhaps more important in the long run, the justices' opinion in the *Gitlow* case also asserted that the free speech and free press protections offered by the First Amendment not only applied to actions taken by the federal government but also to those taken by state governments. Justice Edward Sanford, writing for the majority, asserted, "Freedom of speech and of the press—which are protected by the First Amendment from abridgement by Congress—are among the fundamental personal rights and 'liberties' protected by the due process clause of the Fourteenth Amendment from impairment by the states." This interpretation of the clause in the Fourteenth Amendment guaranteeing "equal protection of the laws" would mark the beginning of the "incorporation" of many of the guarantees of the Bill of Rights into the Fourteenth Amendment, thus preventing the states from acting in ways contrary to those guarantees. In subsequent decades most of the amendments contained in the Bill of Rights—with the exceptions of the Second Amendment's guarantee of the right to bear arms, the Fifth Amendment's guarantee of a defendant's right to have his or her case heard by a grand jury, and the Seventh Amendment's guarantee of a right to a jury trial in civil cases—have come under the protections of the "incorporation doctrine," meaning that state governments are bound by the same constitutional provisions in those cases as the federal government.

Brown v. Board of Education of Topeka (1954). The Supreme Court's unanimous decision to overturn the nearly sixty-year-old "separate but equal" doctrine laid down in *Plessy v. Ferguson* was one of the most momentous decisions ever made by the Supreme Court and indeed one of the most far-reaching steps toward social justice taken by any branch of the federal government.

The case had its origins in a 1951 class-action suit filed by thirteen parents on behalf of their twenty children against the Topeka, Kansas, board of education. The parents, all of whom lived in integrated neighborhoods, attempted to enroll their children in the nearest neighborhood school but were prevented from doing so because those schools were designated for whites only. When the United States District Court for the District of Kansas heard the case, it ruled in favor of the school district, asserting that the quality of the facilities, curriculum, and teachers in the white and African American schools in the district were equal and citing *Plessy v. Ferguson* as precedent for upholding the doctrine of "separate but equal."

The Supreme Court agreed to hear an appeal of the *Brown* case in 1953, along with four similar cases from South Carolina, Virginia, Delaware, and Washington, D.C., and in May 1954 it handed down its ruling. The newly appointed chief justice, former California governor Earl Warren, was well aware of the political and social implications of the case. He not only wrote the opinion in the case but, by careful political and diplomatic maneuvering behind the scenes, persuaded even those justices who may have been reluctant to overturn the long-standing precedent of *Plessy v. Ferguson* to join in a unanimous ruling.

Warren's opinion was, by the standard of many twenty-first-century court opinions, relatively brief, but it was forcefully argued. The central conclusion in Warren's opinion, which went directly against the earlier ruling in *Plessy*, was that even if the quality of the facilities and teachers in the segregated schools was equal, the very fact of segregation was harmful to the African American students and therefore unconstitutional under the equal protection clause of the Fourteenth Amendment. Warren did not support his conclusion solely on the intent of those members of Congress who had framed the Fourteenth Amendment, for he knew that opinions among congressmen on the meaning and scope of the amendment were divided and inconclusive. Instead, he acknowledged that "we cannot turn the clock back to 1868, when the amendment was adopted, or even to 1896 when *Plessy v. Ferguson* was written." Rather, he argued, the court "must consider public education in the light of its full development and its present place in American life." Emphasizing the central importance of education in promoting citizenship and as a road to economic and social success, he concluded that "it is doubtful that any child may reasonably be expected to succeed in life if he is denied the opportunity of an education," and he asserted that education "must be made available to all on equal terms." And then, relying on twentieth-century psychological and sociological studies informed by new knowledge since the *Plessy* decision was rendered, Warren concluded that in the field of public education the doctrine of " 'separate but equal' has no place. Separate educational facilities are inherently unequal."

The Brown decision was the beginning, but hardly the end, of the movement not only to dismantle segregation but also to ensure equal opportunity to minorities in all aspects of American life. The Brown decision could not be implemented by judicial edict alone, and many southern states resisted integrating their schools for many years thereafter. But over the course of the next two decades, the system of state-sponsored segregation of the schools was dismantled, and the move to desegregate the schools gave impetus to a civil rights movement in which Americans, black and white, mobilized to end segregation in all aspects of public life.

The decision in *Brown v. Board of Education* had a few important judicial antecedents, and students of the constitutional debates over equal rights for African Americans might also wish to consult the cases of *Sweatt v. Painter* (1950) and *McLaurin v. Oklahoma State Regents for Higher Education* (1950). Perhaps more important, the constitutional discussion about the meaning of the promise of equality proclaimed in both the Declaration of Independence and the Fourteenth Amendment is still going on today. The Supreme Court, in recent rulings on so-called affirmative action cases (see, for example, *Regents of the University of California v. Bakke*, 1978 and *Grutter v. Bollinger*, 2003), is still trying to find the proper balance between a legal system founded on the principle of equal opportunity and one that prescribes a set of results based on racial categories.

GIDEON V. WAINWRIGHT (1963) AND MIRANDA V. ARIZONA (1966). The civil rights movement of the 1960s, although aimed primarily at securing equal treatment for African Americans, had other ramifications in the legal realm. The emergence of legal aid associations, aimed at securing full legal rights for accused criminals, led to a series of Supreme Court rulings that would, in the first instance, grant additional rights to individuals accused of crimes and, as a consequence, require that law-enforcement officers use greater care in the apprehension, arrest, and questioning of individuals suspected of committing a crime.

The landmark case in this legal revolution was *Gideon v. Wainwright*. The accused in the case, Clarence Earl Gideon, was arrested in Panama City, Florida, on suspicion of having broken into a poolroom, smashed a soda machine, and stolen a small amount of money from a cash register. Although the courts had previously ruled that defendants charged with a capital crime (most often in cases involving the death penalty) were entitled to legal counsel, since this was a case of simple petty larceny the state of Florida ruled that the indigent Gideon was not entitled to court-appointed legal counsel. He attempted to defend himself against the charges, but the jury found him guilty and sentenced him to five years in prison.

Acting on his own behalf, Gideon sought to appeal the decision, claiming that his Sixth Amendment right to a fair trial had been violated by his inability to have competent legal counsel represent him. Against great odds, he was successful in persuading the Supreme Court to hear his case, appointing Abe Fortas, a future Supreme Court justice himself, to defend him. In a unanimous decision, the court ruled that the right to legal counsel was guaranteed by the Sixth Amendment and was "fundamental and essential to a fair trial." Citing the due process clause of the Fourteenth Amendment, the Court, again using the incorporation doctrine, ruled that the constitutional guarantees of the Sixth Amendment should be applied to the actions of the state governments as well as the federal government.

The *Miranda* decision extended the legal rights of accused criminals, but did so in a manner that aroused greater controversy. In that case, Ernesto Miranda was arrested for robbery and later confessed to raping an eighteen-year-old woman a few days before committing the robbery. Miranda's confession, together with a positive identification by the victim, led to his conviction. In a five-to-four ruling, Chief Justice Earl Warren ruled that Miranda's Fifth Amendment rights against self-incrimination had been violated by harsh interrogation techniques and that his Sixth Amendment rights had been violated because he did not have a lawyer present at the interrogation. In Warren's words, a suspect brought in for questioning in connection with a possible crime "must be warned prior to any questioning that he has the right to remain silent, that anything he says can be used against him in a court of law, that he has the right to the presence of an attorney, and that if he cannot afford an attorney one will be appointed for him prior to any questioning if he so desires."

The *Miranda* decision was very controversial at the time that it was handed down, and some continue to complain that it has placed unnecessary constraints on law-enforcement officers in the performance of their duties. However, subsequent Supreme Court decisions have further refined and defined the ways in which an accused's "Miranda rights" might be interpreted, and as police departments have incorporated the principles of the *Miranda* decision into their training manuals, most constitutional scholars and law-enforcement officials have concluded that the *Miranda* decision was on balance an important step forward in America's criminal justice system.

R OE V . W ADE (1973) IS ONE OF THE most controversial cases ever heard by the Supreme Court. The majority opinion, written by Justice Harry Blackmun, held that a woman has a right to terminate her pregnancy—in common parlance, to have an abortion—at any time up until the fetus became "viable," defined as the point at which the fetus has the potential "to live outside the mother's womb." The Court, which supported the majority opinion by a seven-to-two margin, based its ruling on a constitutional "right of privacy." Though nowhere stated in the body of the Constitution or its amendments, privacy was, in the view of the justices, a fundamental right protected by the "due process" clause of the Fourteenth Amendment. Although not all the justices agreed on the matter, at least some justices, and many jurists and scholars subsequently, have believed that the right of privacy is one of the unenumerated rights anticipated in the Ninth Amendment.

The ruling had the effect of invalidating many state laws restricting the right to abortion and setting off a storm of protest, which has not abated even today. Like so many landmark Supreme Court cases, *Roe v. Wade* involved "rights in conflict," the dilemma presented when one set of rights conflicts with another: in this case the freedom of a woman to make her own decisions about whether to terminate a pregnancy and the belief held by many Americans that the fetus—an unborn living being—has a fundamental "right to life." Almost all the Supreme Court cases involving competing sets of rights have the potential to excite controversy, but *Roe v. Wade* moved into particularly volatile territory because the issues involved were not merely legal but also moral and religious, and because the opinions of Americans on those issues were—and continue to be— deeply divided.

In the years since the *Roe* decision was handed down, the Supreme Court has heard several other cases involving the conditions under which state and federal governments might restrict abortions. The effect of these decisions, which include *Planned Parenthood v. Casey (1992)*, *Stenberg v. Carhart* (2000), and *Gonzales v. Carhart* (2007), has been to give governmental entities slightly greater ability to limit the circumstances under which abortions might be performed. For example, in *Planned Parenthood v. Casey* the Court ruled that the state of Pennsylvania might require that doctors provide women contemplating an abortion with information about possible health risks and complications (the doctrine of "informed consent"); that minors seeking an abortion receive consent from a parent or guardian (the doctrine of "parental consent"); and that the state impose a twenty-four-hour waiting period before a woman could proceed with her requested abortion. Given the unsettled state of public opinion on the question of whether and under what circumstances women should be allowed to terminate their pregnancy, it is likely that the Supreme Court will be confronted with further contestation on these issues in the future.

UNITED STATES V. NIXON (1974) WAS A CASE that raised issues relating to the extent and limits of executive power in the name of national security, the nature of executive privilege, and the relationship between the executive and judicial branches in a system of government founded on the principles of separation of power and checks and balances. It is also important in that the judgment in the case had an important impact on an unprecedented event in American history: the resignation of a sitting president, Richard M. Nixon, in the face of near-certain impeachment by the United States House of Representatives.

The facts of the case are part of one of the great political dramas of American history—the so-called Watergate scandal. In June 1972, five burglars, with authorization from Republican Party officials and perhaps President Nixon himself, broke into the Democratic Party headquarters in the Watergate building complex in Washington, D.C., in order to obtain information about George McGovern, President Nixon's opponent in the 1972 presidential election. In the ensuing investigation, seven of President Nixon's close advisers were indicted by a grand jury. In the course of that investigation, it was also discovered that President Nixon had a collection of recorded tapes in his office that would be likely to shed light on whether members of the president's staff—and indeed the president himself—had engaged in a cover-up of the Watergate affair.

President Nixon resisted turning over the tapes, arguing that matters involving national security might be compromised by the release of the tapes and citing "executive privilege" as the basis for his refusal to turn over the full transcripts of the tapes. The question of whether President Nixon should be compelled to turn over the tapes or transcripts was initially heard in the U.S. District Court in Washington, D.C. The court ruled that the president should reveal the full content of the tapes—a decision that Nixon, citing executive privilege, again resisted. The Supreme Court heard the case on July 8, 1974, and handed down its decision on July 24.

The Court ruled unanimously (8–0, with Justice William Rehnquist recusing himself because he had previously served in the Nixon administration) that President Nixon must turn over the tapes. Notably, Chief Justice Warren Burger, who had been appointed to his position by President Nixon in 1969, wrote the majority opinion. Burger did not find that that there were sufficient issues of national security to justify withholding the tapes, nor was he persuaded that issues of separation of powers or of the general need to keep executive communications confidential were sufficient to sustain a claim of "executive privilege." In Burger's words: "Absent a claim of need to protect military, diplomatic, or sensitive national security secrets, we find it difficult to accept the . . . [absolute] confidentiality of Presidential communications."

The immediate effect of the decision in *United States v. Nixon* was to force the resignation of President Nixon, just a few weeks later, on August 9, 1974, because as the content of the Nixon White House tapes was revealed, the president's impeachment by the House of Representatives seemed certain and his conviction by the Senate highly likely. More generally, the decision made it more difficult for any subsequent president to withhold information from other branches of the federal government or from the public simply by asserting the right of executive privilege.

SUGGESTIONS FOR
FURTHER READING

THE VOLUME OF WRITING ON THE ORIGINS, creation, and evolution of the American Constitution is vast, but for the student who wishes to learn more about the particular topics covered in this book, here is a brief listing of some of the most important works written about the American Revolution and Constitution.

THE DECLARATION
OF INDEPENDENCE

The classic work on the drafting and philosophy of the Declaration of Independence is Carl Becker, *The Declaration of Independence: A Study in the History of Political Ideas* (New York: Knopf, 1922). An excellent recent account of the larger context in which the Declaration was forged is Pauline Maier, *American Scripture: Making the Declaration of Independence* (New York: Knopf, 1997). David Armitage, *The Declaration of Independence: A Global History* (Cambridge, MA: Harvard University Press, 2007) views the wider implications of the Declaration of Independence.

THE UNITED STATES CONSTITUTION

The starting point for understanding how the Constitution was created and what the framers of that document intended is the extensive notes kept by James Madison during the Constitutional Convention. Those notes, together with many other documents relating to the creation of the Constitution, can be found in Max Farrand, *The Records of the Federal Convention of 1787*, 4 vols., rev. ed. (New Haven, CT: Yale University Press, 1937, repr. 1966). Jack N. Rakove, ed., *The Annotated U.S. Constitution and Declaration of Independence* (Cambridge, MA: Harvard University Press, 2009) presents extensively annotated versions of both the Declaration of Independence and the Constitution. For an even more detailed analysis of each provision and amendment of the Constitution, see John R. Vile, *A Companion to the United States Constitution and Its Amendments*, 4th edition (Westport, CT: Praeger, 2006). See also Akhil Reed Amar, *America's Constitution: A Biography* (New York: Random House, 2005); and Jack N. Rakove, *Original Meanings: Politics and Ideas in the Making of the Constitution* (New York: Knopf, 1996).

THE FEDERALIST PAPERS

The authoritative scholarly edition, from which the excerpts in this volume are taken, is Jacob Cooke, ed., *The Federalist* (Middletown, CT: Wesleyan University Press, 1966). Among the dozens of works that have analyzed *The Federalist Papers*, a couple of the most useful are David Epstein, *The Political Theory of The Federalist* (Chicago: University of Chicago Press, 1982); and Garry Wills, *Explaining America: The Federalist* (Garden City, NY: Doubleday, 1981).

REVOLUTIONARY ORIGINS

An excellent, brief survey of the revolutionary era is Gordon S. Wood, *The American Revolution: A History* (New York: Modern Library, 2003). Among the most influential works on the American Revolution are Bernard Bailyn, *Ideological Origins of the American Revolution*, enlarged ed. (Cambridge, MA: Harvard University Press, 1992); Robert Middlekauf, *The Glorious Cause: The American Revolution, 1763–1789* (New York: Oxford University Press, 1982); Pauline Maier, *From Resistance to Revolution: Colonial Radicals and the Development of American Opposition to Britain, 1765–1776* (New York: Knopf, 1972); and Gordon Wood, *The Radicalism of the American Revolution* (New York: Knopf, 1992).

THE ARTICLES OF CONFEDERATION

The story of the extraordinary challenges and changes occurring within America during the period between the Declaration of Independence and the framing of the Constitution is best told by Gordon Wood in *The Creation of the American Republic, 1776–1787* (Chapel Hill, NC: University of North Carolina Press, 1969). See also Jack Rakove, *The Beginnings of National Politics: An Interpretive History of the Continental Congress* (New York: Knopf, 1979); and Forrest McDonald, *E Pluribus Unum: The Formation of the American Republic, 1776–1790* (Boston: Houghton Mifflin, 1965).

THE CONSTITUTIONAL CONVENTION OF 1787

The most recent, comprehensive account of the Philadelphia Convention is Richard R. Beeman, *Plain Honest Men: The*

Making of the American Constitution (New York: Random House, 2009). An older, dramatized account is Catherine Drinker Bowen, *Miracle at Philadelphia: The Story of the Constitutional Convention, May to September, 1787* (Boston: Little, Brown, 1966). See also Richard Bernstein, *Are We to Be a Nation? The Making of the American Constitution* (Cambridge, MA: Harvard University Press, 1987); and Clinton Rossiter, *1787: The Grand Convention* (New York: Macmillan, 1966).

RATIFICATION OF THE CONSTITUTION

Merrill Jensen, John Kaminski, and Gaspare Saladino, eds., *The Documentary History of the Ratification of the Constitution*, twenty-one volumes to date (Madison, WI: State Historical Society of Wisconsin, 1976–) have nearly completed the monumental project of publishing the definitive collection of all of the known primary sources relating to the ratification of the Constitution. Secondary works on ratification are Robert Alan Rutland, *The Ordeal of the Constitution: The Antifederalists and the Ratification Struggle of 1787–1788* (Norman: University of Oklahoma Press, 1966); Saul Cornell, *The Other Founders: Antifederalism and the Dissenting Tradition in America, 1788–1828* (Chapel Hill: University of North Carolina Press, 1999); and Michael Allen Gillespie and Michael Lienesch, eds., *Ratifying the Constitution* (Lawrence: University Press of Kansas, 1989).

ESTABLISHING GOVERNMENT UNDER THE CONSTITUTION

Gordon S. Wood, *Empire of Liberty: A History of the Early Republic, 1789–1815* (New York: Oxford University Press, 2009) is a monumental account of the critical early years of the young republic. For an excellent, brief account, see James Roger Sharp, *American Politics in the Early Republic: The New Nation in Crisis* (New Haven, CT: Yale University Press, 1993). George Washington's critically important role in establishing government under the Constitution is discussed in innumerable biographies of America's first president; one of the best is Joseph Ellis, *His Excellency, George Washington* (New York: Knopf, 2004).

THE SUPREME COURT AND THE CONSTITUTION

This is a vast subject area encompassing nearly all aspects of America's history. A few of the notable books among the hundreds on the topic are John A. Garraty, ed., *Quarrels that Have Shaped the Constitution*, rev. ed. (New York: Harper and Row, 1987); Herman Belz, Winifred Harbison, and Alfred H. Kelly, *The American Constitution: Its Origins and Development*, 7th ed. (New York: W.W. Norton, 1991); Joseph F. Menez and John R. Vile, *Summaries of Leading Cases on the Constitution*, 14th ed. (Lanham, MD: Rowman and Littlefield, 2004); Harold Hyman and William M. Wiecek, *Equal Justice Under Law: Constitutional Development, 1835–1875* (New York: Harper and Row, 1982); and William Nelson, *The Fourteenth Amendment: From Political Principle to Judicial Doctrine* (Cambridge, MA: Harvard University Press, 1988).